Unveiling
The Da Vinci Code:
The Mystery of
The Da Vinci Code Revealed,
A Christian Perspective

Unveiling
The Da Vinci Code:

The Mystery of
The Da Vinci Code Revealed,
A Christian Perspective

Bo Kirkwood

All Scripture quotations unless otherwise marked are taken from the New American Standard of the Holy Bible ®, © Copyright 1960,1962,1963, 1968, 1971, 1972, 1973, 1975, 1977, 1995 by The Lockman Foundation. Used by permission.

Printed in the United States of America

Publishing services by Selah Publishing Group, LLC, Arizona. The views expressed or implied in this work do not necessarily reflect those of Selah Publishing Group.

ISBN: 1-58930-164-1
Library of Congress Control Number: 2005937059

Acknowledgements

When deciding whom to acknowledge in the preparation of this book, it became very obvious that the book would not have been possible were it not for the fact that I am a Christian. For this reason, I would like to thank those preachers of the Gospel whose feet I have sat at and have learned so much, some of whom have gone to their reward and others who remain servants of Christ. Such men include: Luther Blackman, the first Gospel preacher I ever heard and the one responsible for the conversions of my mother and father; Ralph Williams, my "father" in Christ; John Iverson; Carl Hollis; David Watts; Tom Roberts; Bill Eckles; Shaddin Edwards; Osby Weaver; and Jerry Fite. I would also like to thank those numerous Gospel preachers I have heard in various lectures, classes, and Gospel meetings over the years from whom I also was edified greatly.

To those men who served as elders in the church I grew up in: Dr. Curtis Torno; Bill Coffey; Alva White; and my departed father-in-law, Don Carter, I owe a great deal of gratitude. Through their exemplary lives and their unbounding zeal for the Gospel and the importance of establishing Bible authority, these men left an indelible impression upon me. I would also like to thank those fellow elders I currently serve with: Bill Lovelace, Chuck McHargue, and Joel Meier for their assiduous desire to stand for the truth.

I would also like to thank those who have proofread my book and offered significant advice and criticism, especially Dub and Sharon Simpson, Dee Bowman, and Jerry Fite.

I must also thank my family for their support over the years. I am blessed to have three wonderful Christian boys, Toby, Danny and Luke, for which I am eternally grateful.

Finally, and most importantly, I would like to thank my best friend and wife, Cherry. This book would truly have been impossible to write without her encouragement, criticism, and help in its preparation. She spent countless hours laboring over the computer in assisting me in researching this book and in the typing of the manuscript.

Bo Kirkwood
Pasadena, Texas

Contents

Foreword

A few months ago, during the course of my travels, I was browsing through an airport bookstore looking for something to read. I had heard about a book called *The Da Vinci Code* by Dan Brown, knew it was a bestseller, and like millions of others, decided to buy the book and read it on my journey. I knew nothing about *The Da Vinci Code* except that it was a bestseller and had something to do with encryptic codes in some of Leonardo Da Vinci's paintings. I also knew that it was a book of fiction and obviously was a bestseller, and, therefore, likely to be a good read.

When I began reading the book, I found it to be both fascinating and difficult to put down. Especially intriguing, in the beginning of the book, Mr. Brown states as fact the existence of two organizations, one being the Priory of Sion and the other the Vatican Prelature, known as Opus Dei. He also states that all descriptions of artwork, architecture, and secret rituals in the book are accurate. This implies that the book, although a book of fiction, is credibly based upon factual material.

As I continued to read the book, which essentially is a murder mystery, it began to unravel some so-called facts through its characters that began to disturb me, as I am sure it did many other readers. I grew up in a Christian environment and have been a Christian for over thirty years. When coming across information purported to be factual that contradicted what I had been taught these many years, I began to have questions.

I knew that many of these details could not be accurate, and after reading the book, I began to do my own research. As a result, I read as many of the critiques on *The Da Vinci Code* that I could find. This led me to read other books that dealt with subjects pertinent to concepts presented in *The Da Vinci Code*, including books on Gnosticism; books on which Dan Brown based some of his work, such as *Holy Blood, Holy Grail*, *The Templar Revelation*, *The Goddess and the Gospels*, and *The Woman with the Alabaster Jar*; as well as other books and articles that appeared in *Time* magazine, *Newsweek*, and *U. S. News & World Report*. I also watched several documentaries that were presented on television regarding *The Da Vinci Code*. As a result of my research, I began to realize that what Mr. Brown had presented in his book as facts were, in fact, distortions, fabrications, and in some cases, out-and-out untruths. For that reason, I felt compelled to write my own critique of *The Da Vinci Code* from a Christian perspective. I, like most of the readers of *The Da Vinci Code*, am not a theologian or art-history expert, but I felt that a book that looks at these issues raised by Mr. Brown's book was important and necessary. I have not tried to duplicate those fine books that have been written regarding *The Da Vinci Code*, but I have tried to present a layman's point of view arranged in a readable and well-organized manner. I would hope readers of this book would also take the time to do their own research and study.

Bo Kirkwood
Pasadena, Texas

1
A Literary Phenomenon

The Da Vinci Code is a twenty-first-century phenomenon. Written by a New Englander and former math teacher, Dan Brown, it has sold more than twenty-five million copies to date, has been translated in forty-four languages, and has been on the top of the *New York Times* bestseller list for over ninety weeks. It continues to be on the bestseller lists since its publication in 2003. The book has spawned an industry unto itself with over ninety related books now in print, as well as a DVD produced by Brigham Young University. In addition to this, tourism has increased in Europe to places mentioned in *The Da Vinci Code,* such as the Louvre museum; the Church of Saint-Sulpice, in Paris; the village of Rennes-Le Chateáu; Westminster Abbey; and finally Rosslyn Chapel, in Scotland. At the time of the printing of this book, *The Da Vinci Code* is also being made into a major motion picture to be directed by Ron Howard with a screenplay by Akiva

Goldman and produced by Brian Grazer. This is the highly successful team that was responsible for the award-winning *A Beautiful Mind*, as well as many other films. Tom Hanks, two-time academy-award winner, will star in the film, which is surely destined to be a mega hit.[1]

U.S. News and World Report predicts that with the success of *The Da Vinci Code*, Mr. Brown will eventually become a billionaire.[2] This is because of the tremendous success of *The Da Vinci Code* itself, sales from a newly published illustrated version of *The Da Vinci Code,* the eventual publication of a paperback version, increased sales of previously produced works by Mr. Brown that were of marginal success, future sales of spin-off books to be written by Mr. Brown that are already in the works, and finally, the predicted success of the afore mentioned movie version.[3] In addition to all of this, Mr. Brown was recently named as one of *Time* magazine's 100 Most Influential People in the World!

And yet *The Da Vinci Code* is a dangerous book. Yes, I said, a "dangerous book." Why would I make such a statement about a work of fiction? At the heart of *The Da Vinci Code* is no less an attempt to undermine the foundation of Christianity. This point was made very clear by Mr. David Klinghoffer in his *National Review* article when he stated, "What's at stake in *The Da Vinci Code* is nothing less than traditional Christianity itself." This is coming from someone who confesses to be a believing Jew! Mr. Klinghoffer also goes on to state, "Any Christian who is offended by fiction that directly contradicts his faith should certainly avoid this book."[4]

Why would Mr. Klinghoffer make such statements about a work of fiction, one would ask? There is no doubt that *The Da Vinci Code* is indeed a work of fiction, and a work of very readable and entertaining fiction at that. The problem is that Mr. Brown presents his book with the idea that contained in his book of fiction are various facts. These facts are presented at the very beginning as they relate to a European secret organization known as the Priory of Sion and the Vatican Prelature, Opus Dei. Mr. Brown also states that, "All descriptions of artwork, architecture, documents, and secret rituals in this novel are accurate."[5] These statements of "fact" give the novel a very strong psychological overtone so the reader is compelled to believe that other "facts" in the book are indeed true.

Furthermore, Mr. Brown himself has come to the conclusion that the premises of the novel are true. In an interview given by Charles Gibson on ABC's *Good Morning America* on November 3, 2003, Mr. Brown stated that after doing his research on the book, although he began as a skeptic, he became, in the end, a "believer." He told Elizabeth Vargas on that same show, "I began as a skeptic. As I started researching *The Da Vinci Code*, I really thought I would disprove a lot of this theory about Mary Magdalene and the Holy Blood and all that. I became a believer."[6]

At this point, if you have not read *The Da Vinci Code*, you may be asking what all the fuss is about. For this reason, I believe it is appropriate to briefly summarize *The Da Vinci Code*, and then look at the questions that arise from this novel.

The story of *The Da Vinci Code* revolves around two central characters: one being Robert Langdon, a Harvard professor and expert in symbolism, and the other being Sophie Neveu, a young cryptologist. Langdon is in Paris on business when a murder occurs in the Louvre museum.

The murder victim, before he dies, leaves a strange cipher, which apparently contains clues about his murderer that Mr. Langdon, being an expert in symbolism, is asked by the Paris police to interpret.

In his quest, he elicits the help of Sophie, the young cryptologist. The murder victim, it turns out, just happens to be Sophie's grandfather, Jacques Sauniere, the curator of the Louvre. Unfortunately for Mr. Langdon, Sophie informs him that he has now become the prime suspect in the murder. As she and Mr. Langdon decipher the code left by Sauniere, they begin to realize that the murder is linked to the legendary search for the Holy Grail. What transpires at this point is a flight from the police by Sophie and Robert Langdon. As a result, and quite by providence, they bump into a character by the name of Sir Leigh Teabing, who has some expert knowledge about the Grail. Through their encounter with Mr. Teabing, Robert and Sophie learn of events that surround the New Testament, including the news that Jesus and Mary Magdalene were secretly married and that the true Holy Grail is, in fact, Mary Magdalene. In fact, Mr. Teabing states: "Almost everything our fathers taught us about Christ is false, as are the stories about the Holy Grail."[7] Teabing also states that the royal bloodline of Jesus Christ has been "chronicled in exhaustive detail by scores of historians."[8] Much of what Teabing believes comes from Gnostic gospels, ancient documents that are supposed to have given a more reliable account of Christ's life and teachings than the New Testament documents we have today. Sir Teabing has in his library four books: *The Templar Revelation: Secret Guardians of the True Identity of Christ; The Woman with the Alabaster Jar: Mary*

Magdalene and the Holy Grail; The Goddess and the Gospel's Reclaiming the Sacred Feminine; and *Holy Blood, Holy Grail,* the acclaimed international bestseller.

Eventually, Robert and Sophie, now in the accompaniment of Sir Leigh Teabing, are forced to flee to London and later Scotland, avoiding the authorities and also in hopes of finding more evidence about the murder and its connection to the Holy Grail. Through their investigation and their meeting with Teabing, Sophie and Robert learn that a secret organization called the Priory of Sion has been in existence for centuries, and its sole purpose has been to hide certain facts about Jesus and Mary Magdalene from the general public. Interestingly, however, through hidden codes, these facts have been kept preserved by Leonardo Da Vinci, who was, at one time, a Grand Master of this secret society. Encrypted in several of his paintings are codes alluding to this mystery of Jesus and Mary Magdalene. On the other side of the equation is a Catholic organization called Opus Dei, which according to the novel, is engaged in attempts to block the Priory of Sion from making public the true relationship between Jesus, Mary Magdalene, and the Holy Grail. As revealed in the novel, Jacques Sauniere was the last Grand Master of the Priory of Sion. He was murdered by a member of Opus Dei at the request of this organization. Of concern to Opus Dei is the location of relics that would divulge these secrets of the Priory and, as a result, expose the Church as being built on fraud and deceit for many centuries. It should come as no surprise that Robert and Sophie never actually find the secret documents of the Priory of Sion. Eventually Robert is exonerated from the murder of Jacques Sauniere. Sophie is reunited with her grandmother and brother, who are discovered to be the last living descendants of Mary Magdalene and Jesus Christ. That is the abbreviated version of *The Da Vinci Code*. If it seems to strain credibility and the premise seems thin, you are not alone in that belief.

The entire scenario begs the question, why would a secret society bent on keeping documents hidden concerning the true nature of Christ and Mary Magdalene be at odds with another organization that has the exact same goal? Supposedly, the Priory is waiting for the right moment in time to reveal such "Sangreal Documents." But in any event, this is the story of *The Da Vinci Code*. It is clear, however, one cannot argue with the success of the novel and the fact that *The Da Vinci Code* is a very compelling read. It is also clear that without the mystery shrouded in Mr. Brown's "broadsides against Christianity,"[9] the book would not be nearly as successful. His sensational claims in the book, although not necessary for the central plot, nonetheless are essential for its success in the public eye.

But again, one asks, "Why so big a deal regarding a book of fiction?" If not for Mr. Brown's statements that his novel is based upon fact, there would not be such criticism. But as we have seen, he has stated that the novel is based upon factual events, factual artifacts, and factual writings.

In truth, *The Da Vinci Code* is more than just a mere mystery novel. Veiled in this novel, and I might add, not so thinly veiled, is a direct attack upon Jesus Christ and His divinity, upon the Church, and upon all those who claim to be followers of Jesus Christ and call Him Savior and Lord. According to Mr. Brown's novel, Christianity was invented to suppress women and to turn people away from the "the divine feminine."[10] He bases this idea on several huge lies and fabrications that have no foundation in truth. The purpose of this book is to expose such fabrications and untruths so the reader will not be uninformed about the true facts.

Make no mistake about it, there is an agenda behind Mr. Brown's book. This agenda is to promote a "pro-feminist" theological viewpoint that seeks to elevate the role of women in the Church, and by doing so, attacks basic fundamental Christian beliefs. Not the least of these is that Jesus was not deity, nor did He claim to be deity, but, in fact, was proclaimed deity centuries after His death by the Council of Nicea, convened by Constantine in 325 A.D. This was all about power, we are told in Mr. Brown's novel, and the Council of Nicea rejected some eighty other viable gospels because they taught Jesus actually wanted Mary Magdalene to be the real leader of the Church.[11] We are also told that in the Old Testament, Israel actually worshipped both a male god, Jehovah, and a feminine counterpart, Shekinah, and it was only centuries later that the "official Church," the supposedly sex-hating, women-hating Church, removed from the Old Testament allusions to goddess worship and eliminated the "divine feminine." We are further taught that Jesus was actually the original feminist, but His wishes were ignored by the early Church in order to propagate a more male-dominated agenda.[12]

Mr. Brown's novel sets forth doctrines and concepts espoused by the Jesus seminars, as well as such "theological scholars" as Karen King of Harvard University Divinity School; Elaine Pagles, a graduate of Harvard Divinity School and now professor at Princeton University; and Margaret Starbird, a New Age theologian, all of whom have attempted to humanize Jesus Christ and deny His true deity, as well as put forth a pro-feminist theological agenda.

The New Testament tells us that Jesus was put on trial by the Roman government. Pontius Pilate, after hearing Jesus proclaim that He had come to "bear witness of the truth," posed the question, "What is truth?"[13]

There are those who would have us now believe that the truth of Jesus Christ is uncertain and each divergent view has equal merit. The question I pose is, "Can we know the truth, and as Christians, should we allow works of such men as Dan Brown to question our faith and undermine the validity of the New Testament Church?" My purpose is to show first that the ideas set forth in *The Da Vinci Code* are based upon fabrications, distortions, and in some cases, out-and-out lies. We will look very closely at Mary Magdalene as portrayed in the New Testament and also as portrayed in Gnostic writings. We will also explore the true purpose of the Council of Nicea, as opposed to that purpose put forth in *The Da Vinci Code*. Because the Gnostic writings are so central and crucial in the theories that have come forth pertaining to Christ and Mary Magdalene, we will look at the Gnostic writings in depth. We will determine if they are indeed equal with the New Testament, if they should be part of the New Testament canon, and if they were considered as part of the New Testament canon by early Christians. We will also look at why such doctrines pertaining to the deity of Jesus Christ would be popular today and why some view Gnosticism as on par with Christianity. Finally, we will answer the question, "Can we really trust the Bible?"

A Literary Phenomenon

Did the early Jews worship a femal goddess, Shekinah?

According to *The Da Vinci Code*, "Early Jews believed that the holy of holies in Solomon's temple housed not only God but also his powerful female equal, Shekinah."[14] *The Da Vinci Code*, through the character Langdon, goes on to say that, "Men seeking spiritual wholeness came to the temple to visit priestesses or hierodules with whom they made love and experienced the divine through physical union."[15] This, of course, is an absurdity. Mr. Brown has stretched the truth significantly in referring to an eleventh- and twelfth-century Gnostic Jewish cult known as the Cabala as "early Jews" to come up with such nonsense. By the time this Jewish cult came into existence, there would not even have been a Solomon's Temple or a Holy of Holies.

First and foremost, the word *shekinah* does not appear in the Bible. The word *shekinah* means "the indwelling presence of God," and comes from the root word *shakah*, which means "to dwell."[16] Certainly, the presence or indwelling of God is found in the Old Testament, but to refer to Shekinah as a goddess is an absolute fabrication. Furthermore, the hierodules that Mr. Brown alludes to in *The Da Vinci Code* were basically female cult slaves and were part of a pagan cult, not a Hebrew cult or Jewish tradition. In fact, such acts described by Mr. Brown are utterly condemned by the Old Testament in Deuteronomy 23.[17] The Jews believed that such immoral acts performed in the Temple would cause the removal of God's presence from that place.

It thus appears that Mr. Brown's claims about Shekinah are based on a misunderstanding of Cabalistic tradition. The Cabala, also spelled Kabbalah, is a very mystical and Gnostic distortion of Jewish theology. They believed that God is manifested in two parts: As He is, and as He is in His manifestation. One part is limitless and "ineffable." The "En Sof" has ten emanations. The division of these emanations, known as "sefirot," can be divided into male and female, with the female principle being called Shekinah. In the Kabbalistic scheme, the sex act between husband and wife becomes a mirror of the divine process on high. But even the Cabalists themselves stressed that the male and female terms referring to the sefirot "should never be understood as references to a goddess or a Pagan notion of Godhead or to some sort of sexual activity on high."[18]

It should be emphasized that this is certainly not early Jewish tradition and such practices are nowhere to be found in the Old Testament. Mr. Brown has completely misrepresented the chronology of events in what appears to be an attempt to "mislead readers and blur the lines between different belief systems."[19]

2
The Unholy Tetralogy

"Nothing in Christianity is original," so says Leigh Teabing in *The Da Vinci Code*.[1] While I believe this to be a false statement, I do believe it can accurately be said that nothing in *The Da Vinci Code* is original. Dan Brown has borrowed very heavily from other sources and alludes to these sources in Chapter 60 of *The Da Vinci Code*. In fact, his treaties on the Priory of Sion and the Holy Grail are taken almost verbatim from the book *Holy Blood, Holy Grail*.

Because *Holy Blood, Holy Grail; Woman with the Alabaster Jar; The Goddess and the Gospels;* and *The Templar Revelation* form such a foundation and inspiration for *The Da Vinci Code*, we will look at each one of these books briefly. *Holy Blood, Holy Grail* was first published in 1982 and written by Michael Bagent, Richard Leigh, and Henry Lincoln, a psychology graduate-photojournalist, a novelist and short-story writer, and a BBC filmmaker, respectively. This book was very successful and highly controversial at the time of its publication, and it forms the foundation of the unholy tetralogy found in Sir Leigh Teabing's library in *The Da Vinci Code*.[2] In fact, most of the hypotheses put forth in *The Da Vinci Code* by Mr. Brown come from *Holy Blood, Holy Grail*. Even the character of Leigh Teabing is named with the last name of one of the authors and an anagram of one of the other author's names: Richard Leigh and Michael Baigent. From this work, Mr. Brown gets his information regarding the Priory of Sion and the theory of the marriage between Jesus and Mary Magdalene. *Holy Blood, Holy Grail* also deals with the mystery of Rennes-Le Chateau (see Appendix I), the Knights Templar, the Merovengian dynasty and bloodline, and the "Holy-Grail hypothesis" alluded to in *The Da Vinci Code*.

Holy Blood, Holy Grail is a convoluted book whose authors make conclusions based on speculation, supposition, and innuendo. It is not a scholarly work. In fact, the authors state that "techniques of academic scholarship were sorely inadequate" in writing their book.[3] They, therefore, took a "comprehensive approach," based on "synthesis," rather than relying on "conventional analysis."[4] Repeated words and phrases such as *perhaps, if, suppose, possibly*, and *it seems to us* appear throughout the book. In his introduction to the paperback version, Henry Lincoln writes that the book was written with a "vision akin to that of a novelist." The authors even go so far as to say, "it is not sufficient to confine oneself exclusively to facts,"[5] in deriving some of their preposterous and outlandish conclusions. As a result, much of their conclusions are based upon myths, legends, and traditions, not on chronicled historical fact. It is easy to see how conclusions such as theirs can be entertained when the facts don't matter! When the facts don't matter, you can prove just about anything.

At the time *Holy Blood, Holy Grail* was written, it was widely condemned by professional historians, and from what is written above, we can be seen why. It is obvious to me that Mr. Brown used this same approach in writing *The Da Vinci Code*.

What is imminently clear about the authors of *Holy Blood, Holy Grail* is their utter disdain for the New Testament. At the end of their book, the authors state that though they are agnostic, when their research led them to Jesus, they approached Him "with what we hoped was a sense of balance and perspective." "We had no prejudices or preconceptions one way or the other, no vested interest of any kind, nothing to be gained by either proving or disproving anything." They further state that they did not believe they had "desecrated or even diminished Jesus in the eyes of those who genuinely revere him."[6] When one looks at the conclusions the authors made, and the sloppy manner in which they arrived at such conclusions, I believe this to be a very disingenuous statement.

The authors clearly have no regard for the New Testament and place more credence in fables, myths, and legends than in the New Testament scriptures. They believe much of the events of the gospel are fabrications and hoaxes. Jesus' crucifixion, for example, was a "staged event" held on private property and in front of a private audience.[7] Further, His resurrection was a complete hoax, and in fact, according to the authors, He probably did not die on the cross anyway. They also enlisted so-called authorities and scholars to support their theories. It would seem that to them, any "authority" or "scholar" is anyone who holds an unproven theory that is contrary to the New Testament, whether they have facts to support them or not.

In their reading of the New Testament, the authors use the same slipshod techniques of supposition, innuendo, and speculation to arrive at their conclusions. The authors misuse the New Testament Scriptures time and time again to promote their agenda. They allude to the many contradictions of the New Testament, but offer no proof of such contradictions. They also have a supreme misunderstanding of the kingship of Jesus Christ. They hold to the same beliefs that most of the Jews of Jesus' day held: Christ had come to establish an earthly kingdom, and they ignore John 18:36, in which Jesus said, "My kingdom is not of this world. If my kingdom were of this world then my servants would be fighting, that I might not be delivered up to the Jews; but as it is my kingdom is not of this realm."

Finally, conclusions made in *Holy Blood, Holy Grail*, to a large extent, are based upon documents placed in the national library of Paris, the Bibliotheque National. These documents include the "Dossiers Secrets" and "Prieure Documents" that were placed in the Bibliotheque National in 1956 by an organization known as the Prieure De Sion or the Priory of Sion. We will look at the Priory of Sion and its documents later in this book, but suffice it to say, most of the conclusions found in *Holy Blood, Holy Grail* stand or fall on the existence and validity of the Priory of Sion and its founders.

Margaret Starbird holds a special honor in *The Da Vinci Code*, as two of her books are found in Sir Leigh Teabing's library. Ms. Starbird wrote *The Woman with the Alabaster Jar: Mary Magdalene and the Holy Grail*, and *The Goddess*

*in the Gospels: Reclaiming the Sacred Feminine. The Woman
with the Alabaster Jar* was published in 1993, and Ms.
Starbird claims that she was inspired by *Holy Blood, Holy
Grail* to write this book.[8] *The Goddess in the Gospels* was
published in 1998 and is basically a follow-up to *The
Woman with the Alabaster Jar.* In it, Ms. Starbird explains
how she derived some of her conclusions in that book.
Before reading *Holy Blood, Holy Grail,* apparently Ms.
Starbird had never entertained the notion that Mary
Magdalene and Jesus Christ were husband and wife. Now
it would seem she is obsessed and fixated on the idea of
"restoring the sacred feminine."[9]

Dan Brown takes his ideas about the sacred feminine
from Margaret Starbird. Also, it is Ms. Starbird who writes
about "Heiros Gammos," an ancient pagan premarital
ritual, and connects this to the anointing of Christ by
Mary of Bethany mentioned in the New Testament.[10] We
will look at this hypothesis later. For now, it should be
noted that for Ms. Starbird's hypothesis to have merit,
Mary of Bethany and Mary Magdalene must be one and
the same person. Unfortunately for her, there is no reason whatsoever to make that assumption when reading
the New Testament.

*The Goddess in the Gospels; Reclaiming the Sacred Femi-
nine* is a very curious book written by Ms. Starbird. Her
stated purpose in writing the book is to satisfy the urg-
ing of her friends to publish "the story of my quest for
the sacred marriage...."[11] In it, Ms. Starbird explains how
she arrives at the hypotheses and conclusions found in
The Woman with the Alabaster Jar.

Ms. Starbird believes she has a prophetic calling to
proclaim that Jesus and Mary were married and restore
the "divine feminine."[12] Her calling is solidified for what

she refers to as "incredible synchronicities," that is, "meaningful coincidences."[13] She further believes she received "direct revelation," as well as "prophetic revelations."[14] She uses an obscure device known as *gemetria* to decipher hidden codes in the New Testament, all of which, interestingly, fit her hypothesis.[15]

Ms. Starbird sees synchronicities in almost everything. She has had "revelations" through these synchronicities concerning such events as the eruption of Mount Saint Helens, the Challenger disaster, and has even seen synchronicities in a leaking toilet![16]

Ms. Starbird also sees allegorical references in many myths, stories, and fairy tales.[17] For example, *Sleeping Beauty, Cinderella, Snow White and the Seven Dwarfs*, and *The Little Mermaid* are all, according to Ms. Starbird, allusions to the sacred feminine. Lest you think I am kidding, Ms. Starbird states that she has been "given the gift of interpreting the symbols and the knowledge" and she "did not have to accept anything as final but rather had the power to rewrite the script as myself."18 Again, as in *Holy Blood, Holy Grail*, the facts don't really matter. As a result of her divine revelation, synchronicities, and her ability to interpret symbols and prophecy, Ms. Starbird has become "certain that Jesus was married and that the woman called Magdalene was his partner, his beloved and his wife."[19]

The final book in Leigh Teabing's library is *The Templar Revelation: Secrets of the True Identity of Christ*, written by Lynn Picknett and Clive Prince. It was published in 1997, and it was also inspired by *Holy Blood, Holy Grail* by Baigent, Leigh, and Lincoln.[20] In large part *The Templar Revelation* rehashes many of the same subjects and hypotheses put forth in *Holy Blood, Holy Grail*, and later by Margaret Starbird, as well. What Mr. Brown does borrow from *The Templar Revelation* is the postulation of secret codes embedded in Leonardo Da Vinci's works *The Last Supper* and *The Virgin of the Rocks*. Otherwise, Ms. Picknett and Mr. Prince continue to buy into the credibility of the Priory of Sion and its documents such as the "Dossiers Secrets." The authors also expound on Ms. Starbird's Heiros Gammos postulation, and Mr. Brown seems to have borrowed from them the notion that the New Testament was written by men who hated women and somehow suppressed sexuality in the New Testament.[21] It is also from *The Templar Revelation* that Mr. Brown postulates that the New Testament was written at the Council of Nicea and contained "the council's own prejudices and agendas."[22] Alas, again, the authors of *The Templar Revelation* are not as concerned about historical facts as they rely on speculations and suppositions to further their agenda.

The Templar Revelation is probably the most blasphemous and heretical book of Sir Teabing's library. It contains hypotheses that any loyal Christian could only view as sacrilegious. The authors believe Jesus and John the Baptist were rivals and that John was eventually murdered by the disciples of Christ because of John's increasing popularity.[23] They also believe Jesus learned magic in Egypt and His miracles were nothing more than cheap tricks and illusions. Furthermore, Jesus borrowed from the Egyptians their mythology concerning their gods, Orisis and Isis, and even staged His supposed death and resurrection to conform to this mythology.[24] Mary Magdalene was a "sexual initiatrix" in the tradition of the temple prostitute and represented the goddess Isis on earth. According to the authors, she and Jesus conspired to perpetuate the Egyptian mythology. The authors take their hypothesis from two very suspect works: *The Passover Plot* written by Hugh Schonfield, published in 1984, and Morton Smith's *Jesus the Magician* published in 1978. Just like the book *Holy Blood, Holy Grail, The Templar Revelation* is not particularly scholarly. It treats fringe works, such as those cited above, with more respect than academic works. In fact, the authors treat true academics and scholars with scorn and contempt!

Their prejudice against the New Testament is blatantly obvious. Repeatedly, they refer to the New Testament as "propaganda." Paul's fellow ministers are referred to as "henchmen," and Peter is claimed to have hated women.[25] They talk about the "glaring contradictions" in the New Testament,[26] but they obviously have an extreme misunderstanding of biblical interpretation. Yet, they do like to pick and choose what parts of the Bible they consider to be factual.

A point should be made about "the Church." Picknett and Prince along with many other writers make the mistake of equating the New Testament Church with the Catholic Church. They are not the same!

What we know as the Roman Catholic Church did not come into existence until centuries after the establishment of the Church on the day of Pentecost. The Catholic Church is in fact, the "Apostate Church," and the origins of the apostacy were brewing in the first century. Paul warned of this in his second letter to the Thessalonians.

The Roman Catholic Church bears no resemblance to the Church described in the New Testament. First, its organization is different. In the first century, there was no central organization as we see in the Catholic Church, but rather each church was autonomous, having a multiple of elders or bishops serving only that local church. Second, the Roman Catholic Church practices and believes things that are nowhere to be found in the New Testament. Such things include the office of a pope, infant baptism, the perpetual virginity of Mary, purgatory, the division of clergy and laity, and a host of other false doctrines.

No doubt the Roman Catholic Church eventually dominated Christianity, but once again, I believe it is a mistake to equate Roman Catholicism with the New Testament Church. They simply are not the same.[27]

The essence of Picknett and Prince's opinion on Christianity can be seen in their view of Christ. They view Jesus as nothing more than a pagan imposter who "entertained people with his magic."[28] He, along with John the Baptist and Mary Magdalene, preached Gnosticism and baptized disciples in an "ancient occult tradition" with the supreme initiation coming through "sexual ecstasy."[29] It cannot be overemphasized that this is one of several books that Dan Brown apparently researched in his writing of *The Da Vinci Code*!

As stated earlier, it is from *The Templar Revelation* that Mr. Brown finds the idea of secret codes being hidden in Leonardo's *The Last Supper* and *The Madonna (Virgin) of the Rocks*. His discussion in *The Da Vinci Code* of these works comes straight from Picknett and Prince, who believe that Leonardo was a strong Johnite. It is also from *The Templar Revelation* that the discussion in *The Da Vinci Code* comes concerning the Council of Nicea. Also from *The Templar Revelation*, Mr. Brown derives the idea of "secret relics" being hidden somewhere in Europe that would prove that Mary Magdalene and Jesus were married.[30] Of this point, Picknett and Prince differ with the authors of *Holy Blood, Holy Grail*. They believe the real agenda behind the "Priory of Sion" is keeping these relics safe and secure, whereas the authors of *Holy Blood, Holy Grail* buy into the stated purpose of the Priory, that is proving the existence of the Merovengian bloodline, the rightful heirs to the throne of France. Two points must be stated. First, both groups of authors believe in the true nature of the Priory of Sion. Second, at no time have the original officers of the Priory stated they believe the Merovengians came from the lineage of Jesus and Mary.

Finally, it is from the *Templar Revelation* that Mr. Brown may have come up with the Opus Dei hypothesis. Although Opus Dei is not mentioned by Picknett and Prince, they do believe that the Catholic Church has kept hidden from Christians certain "facts" concerning Christ and Christianity for centuries in order to maintain the status quo.[31]

What is never really investigated by Picknett and Prince is the problem of motivation. What motivated Christ, John the Baptist, and Mary Magdalene? The stated motive by the authors is political. In other words, Jesus' ministry was really a ploy for setting up a devout following and eventually establishing a kingship on earth. This is obviously a flawed concept. First, Jesus taught repeatedly that His kingdom was not of this world.[32] Second, Jesus taught a religion of peace and of love. Jesus taught to love one's enemies and treat one's neighbors as oneself.[33] His teachings smack against a political agenda. Further, if Christ staged His own crucifixion, as the authors of *The Templar Revelation* attest, and as a result survived, what happened to Him? They offer no good explanation as to why Jesus' political ploy failed, yet

His religion flourished well after His death. The bottom line is, the ideas put forth in *The Templar Revelation* are sheer nonsense!

So, it can be seen that most of Mr. Brown's hypotheses emanate from others. What does seem to be original with Mr. Brown is the inclusion of the secretive Catholic organization Opus Dei in the conspiracy. As previously stated, Mr. Brown may have gotten his notion from *The Templar Revelation*, but I am not totally convinced that even he believes Opus Dei exists to squelch any hidden revelation concerning Jesus Christ and Mary Magdalene.

In one sense, it is hard to blame Mr. Brown for all the inaccuracies and falsifications that he presents in his book. Nonetheless, when he professes to have done two years of research in writing his book, he must indeed shoulder the blame. Much of Mr. Brown's "research" involved reading some very suspect books with very poor scholarly research, and swallowing their faulty conclusions hook, line, and sinker.

In the next chapter, we will look at several topics that occur in *The Da Vinci Code* that I believe to be very suspect, and in some cases to be fraudulently portrayed. It is not my intent to cover all the inaccuracies and lies in *The Da Vinci Code* (and there are many). Besides, that has been done quite well by others. Instead, we will look at those issues that are crucial to the story as they relate to Christianity and the Church. In the next chapter we will answer the questions: Is the Priory of Sion real? Were the Knights Templar created by the Priory of Sion to protect secret Sangreal documents? What is Opus Dei? And, did Leonardo Da Vinci put encryptic codes in his paintings?

3
When the Fact Don't Matter

Is the Priory of Sion real? Well, yes and no. Yes, there was and maybe still is a secret society by the name of the Priory of Sion, but no, there is no evidence it existed before 1956, when the Priory registered and submitted statutes of organization with the government of France.[1] In fact, the Priory of Sion would appear to be a great hoax concocted by a rather shadowy ex-con and anti-Semite, Pierre Plantard, and some of his cronies.[2]

Pierre Plantard, who took on the name Pierre Plantard De Saint-Clair, is a rather shadowy figure and is mentioned prominently in *Holy Blood, Holy Grail* and *The Templar Revelation*. Mr. Plantard is the apparent mastermind behind the Priory of Sion and was allegedly its last grand master. He was born in 1920 in France, and in 1942, during the occupation by the Nazis, wrote a journal called *Conquest for Young Knighthood* (*Vaiencre pour una jeune chevaleric*), which was "markedly uncritical of the Nazi oppressors."[3] It was through Pierre Plantard, under the alias "Captain Way," that the committees of public safety in France eventually would bring about the return of power of General Charles de Gaulle in 1958. Pierre Plantard was also responsible for editing *Circuit*, a magazine of the Priory. Mr. Plantard wrote under the pseudonym "Chyren" for the magazine, which was mostly devoted to esoteric matters.[4]

In *Holy Blood, Holy Grail*, the authors seem somewhat enamored with Pierre Plantard. In interviews with Mr. Plantard, the authors noted that he was unwilling to say anything about the activities of the Priory of Sion or its objectives.[5] They did notice certain "curious inconsistencies" in his interview and stated that he seemed to speak with two voices, one being that of the Sion's Secretary General and the other of an "incognito king." They themselves even considered dismissing the Priory as a "minor lunatic fringe sect, if not an outright hoax."[6]

Through the Priory's literature, it becomes obvious that the real purpose of the Priory of Sion was to promote Pierre Plantard as heir to a bygone royal French bloodline, the Merovengians, who were once kings in what is now part of France. The Merovengian kings began ruling in the fifth century, the first being King Clovis. In essence, Mr. Plantard was claiming himself to be the rightful heir of a now defunct kingship.

Concerning the "Dossiers Secret" that Dan Brown mentions in *The Da Vinci Code*, they also do exist. They were placed in the national library of France in the 1960s and are twentieth-century typewritten materials! They certainly are not on old parchment as claimed by *The Da Vinci Code*.

Unfortunately for Mr. Plantard, there was a falling-out with some of his co-conspirators, namely a Gerard de Sade and Phillipe de Cherisey, and the Priory was exposed as a hoax. In fact, Andre Bonhomme, the original president of the Priory, stated in a 1996 BBC special that the Priory was "four friends who came together to have fun."[7] One would have to assume that either Mr. Brown did not research this information in the writing of his book or he chose to ignore it.

As far as the Priory hiding the secret documents that revealed Mary Magdalene and Jesus to be married, even Pierre Plantard himself disavowed this notion. Again, Mr. Plantard's purpose was to "prove" that the Merovingians were the rightful heirs to the throne of France, even though France was no longer a monarchy.[8] In fact, there is no evidence that the Merovingian bloodline even continues to exist.

Is there a still a Priory of Sion? Mr. Plantard is now deceased and he was the last known "grand master." No one at this point has laid claim as the new grand master.[9] What seems abundantly clear is that Leonardo Da Vinci, Isaac Newton, Robert Boyle, Victor Hugo, Claude Debussy, and Botticelli were never grand masters of some secret organization known as the Priory of Sion.

A few points should be made. First, what seems to have confused some is the Order of the Priory of Sion, which *did* exist in the Holy Land during the Middle Ages. There is no evidence, however, that this organization continued on into the twentieth and twenty-first century, and it is certainly not related to the Priory of Sion mentioned in *The Da Vinci Code*. Also, when asked in a National Geographic Special whether or not he thought the Priory was real, Mr. Brown was somewhat coy in his answer, basically saying that he was not sure, but he "believed it was."[10]

Knights Templar

The Knights Templar play an important role in *The Da Vinci Code*. According to Mr. Brown, the Knights Templar was founded by the Priory of Sion to locate the secret "Sangreal Documents" that were supposedly in Jerusalem, and then guard those documents, which proved that Jesus was married to Mary Magdalene. According to Mr. Brown, eventually Pope Clement, in order to prevent the release of the information contained in these documents, devised an "ingeniously planned sting operation,"[11] arresting all of the Templar Knights and burning them at the stake.

The Knights Templar were indeed a real organization. They were born during the period of the Crusades, and their intention was to protect pilgrims going to the Holy Land during that time. They were founded in 1118, and they referred to themselves as "poor fellow soldiers of Jesus Christ." They were a unique group of individuals who were both warriors and monks. Those who volunteered to join the Knights Templar were required to take vows and donate all of their possessions to the Templar organization. They also were required to cut their hair and refrain *from* cutting their beards. Furthermore, they were not allowed to retreat from battle and were required to fight to the death if necessary. King Baldwin II provided lodgings for this group of new monk warriors at the Temple Mount, or "the Dome of the Rock," which they named *Templum Domini*, supposedly on the location of Solomon's temple; hence, their name became known as the Knights Templar.

In 1139 Pope Innocent II issued a Papal Bull that stated that the Knights Templar were totally independent of secular and sacred governments, and, therefore, exempt from paying taxes. As a result of this and also due to vast donations given to them, the Knights Templar became a very wealthy organization. They came to own their own seaports and founded the first international banking system. They also built gothic cathedrals, including the Cathedral of Notre Dame in Paris.

In 1291, the Crusades concluded with the fall of the fortress at Acre to the Saracens. This should have been the last hurrah for the Knights Templar, but by this time, they had become so powerful and financially wealthy that they continued on.

By 1306, their wealth had grown so much that King Phillip IV of France, also known as Phillip the Fair, became desperate for their riches. He owed large sums of money and was aware that the Templars' influence was now greater than his own. As a result, he began to do what he could to destroy the Knights Templar. When Pope Boniface VIII would not follow Phillip's order to be rid of the Knights Templar, he had him caught and murdered. The next Pope, Benedict XI, also died very suspiciously soon after becoming Pope. King Phillip was able to persuade Pope Clement to denounce the Knights Templar, and as a result, had them arrested and accused of heresy, necromancy, blasphemy, homosexuality, and other crimes against the Church. As a result, many were tortured and murdered. In 1314, the last grand master of the Templars, Jacques de Molay, was burned at the stake.

Not all Templars were murdered; some survived, especially in Scotland where the Papal Bull was largely ignored. The Templars there eventually became aligned with the Scottish royal bloodline, the House of Stuart. When the House of Stuart was exiled into France, they became involved with "free masonry," and what is now known as Scottish Right Free Masonry had its origins at that time.

Nowhere in historical documents, other than the documents that occur in the "Dossier Secret"—which we previously noted, were placed in the national library of France in 1956 by the Priory of Sion—are the Priory and Templar Knights connected. Furthermore, any connection between the Knights Templar and the search for the "Holy Grail" is speculation and fiction, and would be more appropriately found in a Monte Python movie than in a book of history. So, it is apparent that the Knights Templar existed in history. But again, there is no historical connection between them, the Priory of Sion, and the "Holy Grail."[12]

Opus Dei

In *The Da Vinci Code*, Opus Dei is the secretive Catholic organization that is involved in trying to find the Sangreal documents and keep them from being brought forth to the public. The character Silas is a member of this organization and is working for Aringarosa, the leader of Opus Dei.

Obviously, these characters are fictional, but the organization Opus Dei is not. It is, indeed, a "Prelature" of the Catholic Church, and its full name is "Prelature of the Holy Cross and Opus Dei."

Opus Dei exists today and reports to have an estimated 80,000 to 90,000 members worldwide, with as many as 30,000 to 50,000 in the United States. It was founded in Spain in 1928 by Monsignor Josemaria Escrivá de Balaguier. Monsignor Balaguier was sainted in 2002, just twenty-seven years after his death, by Pope Paul II.

Opus Dei's stated mission is "to contribute to that evangelizing mission of the Church. Opus Dei encourages Christians of all social classes to live consistently with their faith, in the middle of ordinary circumstances of their lives, especially through the sanctification of their work."[13] Members do not necessarily have to be Catholic, nor do they have to be male, to join Opus Dei. Those who do join can be part of two types of membership: the Supernumery and the Numery. Supernumery members make up about 70 percent of the organization, and they concentrate on the sanctification of their work and family duties. Numeries compose the other portion of Opus Dei, and they pledge celibacy and donate their entire possessions and income to the organization. As a result of this, most of the Numery class live in Opus Dei houses that are scattered throughout the world, one of which is in New York City at the corner of Lexington and 34th Street.

The Numery members give up most of their personal freedom when they become members. In fact, entertainment is strictly controlled and censored. Books must be approved by the director, and members can watch TV only in the company of a chaperone. Also, movement in and out of the Opus Dei residencies is strictly monitored and subject to permission from the member's director.

Opus Dei has come under much criticism and controversy, especially for its practices of recruitment, and also the practice of corporal mortification. Some have accused

Opus Dei of brainwashing its members and using recruitment tactics that are somewhat underhanded and suspicious. Also, the practice of corporal mortification is a routine part of a Numery's daily life. Corporal mortification sometimes involves the use of the "cilice," as depicted by the character Silas in *The Da Vinci Code*. A "cilice" is a spiked chain that is worn around the upper thigh and produces pain to the individual. It is apparently obligatory for the Numery members to wear it about two hours a day and at other specific times.

Needless to say, Opus Dei is highly critical of Dan Brown's interpretation of the Bible in general, as well as of their own organization in particular, and has fought back against what they consider unfounded characterizations. Certainly, the idea that Opus Dei is involved in searching for some secret "Sangreal Documents" and attempting to keep them from the public is pure fiction.

Leonardo Da Vinci

Leonardo da Vinci is central to the book *The Da Vinci Code*. According to Dan Brown's book, the artist encrypted secret codes into his paintings, which are paramount to the story and the basis for this novel. He is supposedly one of the grand masters of the Priory of Sion and, therefore, responsible for perpetuating the secret of the Holy Grail. Three of his works are mentioned in Mr. Brown's book: *Madonna (Virgin) of the Rocks, The Last Supper,* and the *Mona Lisa*. We will look at each one of these works and the claims of the Secret Codes in *The Da Vinci Code*. But before that, a brief introduction to Leonardo da Vinci is appropriate.

Leonardo da Vinci was born in 1452 in the Tuscan village of Vinci. The surname "da Vince" is in actuality a description indicating the location of Leonardo's origins. Leonardo da Vinci has come down through the ages to personify genius. He was a true Renaissance man and the epitome of intellect. He was a painter, sculpture, architect, musician, mathematician, engineer, scientist, and inventor. He drew the earliest rendition of flying machines, tanks, the parachute, the car, and the helicopter, which would not come to fruition for centuries. He drew anatomical studies of the human body, which have contributed to the study of medicine even today. Although he was not as a prolific a painter as Dan Brown would have us to believe, Leonardo did paint some of the most remarkable works of art in existence today. The *Mona Lisa*, for example, is the most viewed painting in the world, and possibly the most valued painting in the world.

Leonardo was born the illegitimate son of a peasant girl. In 1466, at the age of fourteen, he moved to the Italian city of Florence. He was an apprentice under Andrea del Verrocchio from whom he learned painting, sculpture, and technical mechanical arts. He painted the *Madonna (Virgin) of the Rock* in 1483, and in 1499, he painted *The Last Supper*, commissioned by Duke Ludovico Sforza for the refectory wall of his family chapel and burial place, the Santa Marie delle Grazie in Milan. In 1502, Leonardo entered the service of Cesare Borgia, the Duke of Valentinois. Leonardo served as a military engineer for the Duke, and it was there that he met the famous Machiavelli, the Italian author and statesman. It was in 1502 that Leonardo painted the portrait of Madonna Lisa, the wife of Francisco del Giocondo. Although Leonardo never named his portrait, it would later become known as the *Mona Lisa*. Leonardo da Vinci died on May 2, 1519. In total, he would paint seventeen works of art during his lifetime, completing only four.

Much has been said about the personal life of Leonardo da Vinci. He was never married and had a predilection for young male students, which have led some to conclude that he was a homosexual. He was anonymously accused twice for sodomy in Florence while living with the painter Rutchio. These accusations were never substantiated, and the charges were eventually dropped. Such accusations could have been politically motivated, because the same accusations were leveled at members of the Medici clan during this time. There are certainly many mysteries that surround the life of Leonardo da Vinci. There are, however, no mainstream scholars who tie Leonardo da Vinci to the Priory of Sion, and there are no mainstream historians who characterize Leonardo's painting as containing encrypted codes to be interpreted in later eras. Such speculations make for interesting and intriguing works of fiction, but they have no basis in fact. Let's look briefly at the three works of art that are mentioned in Dan Brown's book.

The first, *Madonna (Virgin) of the Rocks* has two versions. One, painted in 1483, is alluded to in Mr. Brown's book, and hangs at the Louvre museum in Paris. The second version was painted in 1506 and now hangs in the National Gallery in London.

Before discussing the painting, it is important to understand the theory behind its misinterpretation. For this, Mr. Brown relies heavily on the Templar Revelation for his theory. The theory is as follows: Supposedly Leonardo da Vinci was a Johnite. Johnites believe that John the Baptist and Jesus were rivals with one another; that is, they were competing with each other for disciples. To a Johnite, John the Baptist would be of at least equal importance as Jesus Christ, if not more, and thus more "blessed." History indicates there were people of the Middle Ages who revered John the Baptist, and many portraits of John the Baptist were painted, including Leonardo's last unfinished painting. What cannot be proven, however, is that Leonardo da Vinci was a Johnite. With these facts in mind, let's consider the painting.

The original version of the *Madonna (Virgin) on the Rocks* was actually commissioned by the monks of the Confraternity of the Immaculate Conception for the Church of San Francisco Grande in Milan, and not by nuns, as Mr. Brown states in his book. In the painting, there is a blue-robed Mary, mother of Jesus, with her arm around an infant who is in a praying gesture to another smaller infant that is under the hand of the angel, Uriel. Mr. Brown assumes that the child whose hand is clasped in prayer is Jesus praying to John. Furthermore, he believes that Mary was holding a rather menacing hand over the head of the smaller infant, who is identified by Mr. Brown as John. Finally, he states that Uriel is making a cutting gesture with his hand as if "slicing the neck of the invisible head gripped by Mary's claw-like hand."[14] Unfortunately for the readers, Mr. Brown has misread the work of Leonardo de Vinci's confusing the figure of John the Baptist with Christ and vice versa. In fact, Mary's hand is suspended over her own son, Jesus Christ, with her right hand embracing Christ's cousin, John, who is actually kneeling in reverence and paying homage to Christ. John the Baptist was the first to recognize Christ's divinity while even in the womb of his mother, Elizabeth, as told in the first chapter of Luke. Mr. Brown, therefore, has twisted the true meaning of the painting.

It was mentioned earlier that the *Mona Lisa* was painted in 1503 and was commissioned by Francisco del Giocondo as a portrait of his wife, Madonna Lisa. In an interview for a National Geographic special, Mr. Brown stated that the portrait *Mona Lisa* looks neither male nor female but is an "androgynous self-portrait of Leonard da Vinci." He apparently arrives at this conclusion from research done by two individuals—Lillian Schwartz of Bell Labs and Dr. Digby Quested of the Maudsley Hospital in London, who demonstrated that the *Mona Lisa* could be interpreted as a self-portrait by morphing a famous self-portrait of Leonardo da Vinci as an old man with the portrait of the *Mona Lisa*. This may be fascinating, but it is extremely speculative, to say the least.

Robert Langdon in Mr. Brown's book further makes the absurd statement that the *Mona Lisa* is an anagram whose letters can be rearranged to form the word *Amon L'isa*. Amon refers to the god of masculine fertility in the Egyptian culture, and L'isa stands for the female goddess Isis, whose ancient pictogram was once called L'ise. There are two problems with this notion, however. First, Leonardo da Vinci never named the portrait during his lifetime. Second, the work *Mona Lisa* is actually a contraction for the work *Monna* or *Mia Donna* meaning "my lady" or "madam."[15] The English rendition of the *Mona Lisa* is most likely a spelling error that occurred sometime in the past. These facts do not fit Mr. Brown's agenda, and I suppose were missed in his research.

The most important painting of Leonardo da Vinci alluded to by Mr. Brown is the painting of *The Last Supper.* Through the character Teabing in *The Da Vinci Code*,[16] he stated that *The Last Supper* practically shouts at the viewer that Jesus and Magdalene were "a pair": *The Last Supper* was commissioned by Duke Ludovico and is a fresco painted on the refectory wall of Santa Maria delle Grazie in Milan, Italy. It may very well be Leonardo's most famous work and was considered so even in his own day. The painting on the wall of the refectory measures about fifteen by twenty-nine feet and is painted in a thick layer of egg tempra on top of dry plaster. It began deteriorating, unfortunately, just years after it was painted, and at this point in time, is in a bad state of repair. It was badly damaged in World War II and very little of the original paint exists today. Restoration was carried out in 1954, but it was almost impossible to recreate the exact images and expressions on the faces of the apostles and Jesus and restore the painting to its original state.

Mr. Brown would have his readers believe that the person sitting just to the right of the central character, Jesus Christ, represents Mary Magdalene. His supposition for this is the very feminine characteristics this figure displays. He would further point out that the "V" formed by the separation from Jesus and the character to his right is the symbolic representation of the feminine. In an interview with Elizabeth Vargus for *Primetime Monday*, Mr. Brown stated, "The symbol here is essentially the womb in its very strict, symbolic sense."[17] Also, the mirror images of the supposed Magdalene and Christ can be seen to form the letter *M*, which represents "Magdalene" in Mr. Brown's hypothesis. Further, according to author Brown, *The Last Supper* shows Peter leaning "menacingly toward Mary Magdalene and slicing his blade-like hand across her neck." Finally he alludes to a dagger that is not attached to a hand as an ominous gesture to destroy Mary Magdalene.[18]

As in the case of the *Mona Lisa*, there are many problems with Mr. Brown's theory. First of all, if *The Last Supper* is a depiction of Christ and His twelve disciples, and if Mary Magdalene is also included in this painting, then we are obviously missing another apostle somewhere. Who that apostle is and the reasoning for his not being accounted for would be a significant question. Second, while the figure to the right of Jesus Christ does appear to have some feminine characteristics, it should be pointed out that there are other figures in the painting who also do not show facial hair and could be viewed as "feminine." Third, if the figure to Jesus Christ's right is the apostle John, as most scholars believe it to be, it was not unusual during the Renaissance period for the apostle John to be depicted with feminine characteristics.[19] It should also be pointed out that, as already mentioned, the painting of *The Last Supper* began deteriorating very shortly after it was painted, and the picture that we have now may not be much more than a smudged reproduction of what was there to begin with. Also, there is no supposed disembodied hand as Dan Brown suggests. The knife is being held by Peter, although admittedly in a somewhat awkward fashion. As far as the figures of Christ and Mary forming the letters V and M, there is no logical reason to make those assumptions. In Renaissance art, perspective was very important. The apostles were actually grouped in a triangular fashion and in four triangular groupings. Jesus was centrally placed in a prominent posture, emphasizing His importance so that the observer will immediately gravitate to that position.[20]

In reality, *The Last Supper* was painted to emphasize the betrayal of Christ that was about to occur through one of His apostles, Judas Iscariot. It memorializes that time in history when Christ instituted the Lord's Supper just prior to His crucifixion, which all the Gospels portray. There is no evidence at all that the painting is encoded with a secret message to be perpetuated through the eras indicating that Mary Magdalene was at the right hand of Christ and intended to be head of His Church after His death.

4
Mary Magdalene:
Disciple of Christ or
Priest Goddess of Isis

Much of Dan Brown's book *The Da Vinci Code* hinges around the character of Mary Magdalene. Mr. Brown claims through his character Leigh Teabing that Mary Magdalene was the heir apparent to Christ. He further claims that this was suppressed by the early fathers of Christianity, who were male chauvinists. Mr. Teabing also states that winners write history and these fathers of Christianity won; therefore, the history of Mary's importance has been changed, and the New Testament reflects this male-dominant point of view.[1]

As stated earlier, according to *The Da Vinci Code*, Mary Magdalene was secretly married to Christ, bore Him a child, and fled to what is now France to protect the lineage of Christianity. Apparently, this was to enable a kingdom to be established at a later time through the lineage of Christ. This scenario is severely flawed. First, there is no evidence that Mary was married to Christ, but even more so, there is no evidence that Christ intended for any one person to be the head of His Church on earth. The book of Ephesians states precisely that Christ is the head of the Church.[2] Some have misused Matthew 16 to try to show that Peter was to be the head of the Church. In this passage, Peter was asked by Christ, "But who do you say I am?" Peter answered, "Thou are the Christ, Son of the Living God." Jesus then said, "Blessed are you Simon Barjona, because flesh and blood did not reveal this to you, but my Father who is in heaven, and I also say to you that you are Peter, and upon this rock I will build my Church, and the gates of Hades shall not overpower it."[3] In this passage, Jesus was not proclaiming that Peter would be the *head* of His Church, but it is *his confession* that Christ is the Son of the Living God that would be the foundation, or the rock, upon which the Church would be built. All those who belong to Jesus Christ must believe that He is the Son of the Living God.

Also, there is a misunderstanding concerning the nature of the kingdom of Jesus Christ. Christ said in the gospel of John, "My kingdom is not of this world."[4] It was never Jesus' intent to establish an earthly kingdom. The Jews of His day did not understand this, and, unfortunately, many so-called Christians today do not understand this, either. Christ's kingdom was established, and John preached in Matthew that the kingdom of heaven was at hand.[5] Jesus Christ did come to set up a kingdom, and that kingdom is a spiritual kingdom, His Church. It was established in Acts 2 on the Day of Pentecost.[6]

Who Was Mary Magdalene?

Dan Brown's ideas concerning Mary Magdalene are not original. He takes them from multiple sources, not the least of which are several leading radical feminist theologians such as Elaine Pagels, Margaret Starbird, Karen King, and Lynn Picknett, to name a few. Ms. Pagels's books include *The Gnostic Gospels, Beyond Belief,* and *Adam and Eve and the Serpent.* Karen King has written, *What Is Gnosticism?* and *The Gospel of Mary Magdela: Jesus and the First Woman Apostle.* These radical theological feminists, as well as many others, have an agenda that is no less than to destroy orthodox Christianity. They accept Gnostic writings as equal to the New Testament writings. They believe that Mary Magdalene was "an apostle to the apostles," and was picked by Jesus to carry on Christianity after His death. Most of these feminists do not believe that Christ was really the Son of God, and most do not believe in His resurrection. To prove my point, in an interview with Dan Burstein in his book, *Secrets of the Codes,* Margaret Starbird is quoted as saying that she did not think styling Mary Magdalene as an apostle, equal to the twelve apostles, or "perhaps even more important than Peter" goes nearly far enough. "There is no doubt that Mary Magdalene shows total devotion and faithfulness to Christ, but the gospels tell a different story. In the earliest Christian text, Mary Magdalene is not merely equal in status to Peter. She is defined as the archetypal bride of the eternal bridegroom and provides the model for the quest and desire of the human soul (and the entire human community) for the union with the Divine. She models the way of 'eros' relatedness, the way of the heart, and together with her bridegroom provides the paradigm for imaging the Divine as partners. Her role as an apostle or emissary 'fades in comparison.'"[7] Ms. Starbird goes on to say that "clearly the woman with the alabaster jar who anointed the ancient archetype, was immediately recognized in every corner of the Roman empire." She is alluding to an ancient right of hieros gamos, where the royal bride "proclaimed and even conferred kingship of her anointing of the bridegroom."[8] Clearly, this also assumes that the woman with the alabaster jar was Mary Magdalene, though the Bible claims that the woman was Mary of Bethany.

Lynn Picknett also believes that the woman with the alabaster jar who anointed Jesus was carrying out a pagan right and not a Jewish custom that involved anointing a chosen man, both on the "head and feet—and also on the genitals—for a very special destiny."[9] She further claims that the anointing of the sacred kind in which the priestess singled out the chosen man and anointed him, before bestowing his destiny before him in a sexual rite known as *hieros gamos* (sacred marriage). "Without the power of the woman, the chosen could never reign and would be powerless. This was the original meaning of 'holy matrimony' *hieros gamos*...."[10]

One might ask, at this point, where do these individuals come up with such absurd ideas when they are nowhere to be found in the New Testament? For that, these so-called theologians refer to the Gnostic gospels, and indeed, without the Gnostic gospels, much of their ponderings could be more easily dismissed. We will deal with Gnostism more extensively in another chapter, but for our purposes here, suffice it to say that even if the "Gnostic gospels" are on a par with the New Testament (which I certainly do not believe), they do not, as Lynn Picknett says in her book *Mary Magdalene*, "overwhelmingly suggest Jesus and Mary Magdalene were committed and passionate lovers."[11] In actuality, in all the Gnostic writings, there are only two references to Jesus and Mary of Magdala. One occurs in the Gospel of Phillip where

Mary is described as a companion of Jesus,[12] and the other in the Gospel of Mary, where Mary Magdalene is described as having a special revelation given to her by the Savior.[13] Even in these two instances, it is never stated that Mary was married to Jesus and certainly nowhere is it stated that she was pregnant with Jesus' child. In the chapter on the Gnostics, we will look in greater detail at gnostic theology and cosmology, and this so-called Christian sect.

Mary Magdalene of the New Testament

We shall now turn to what the Bible does say about Mary Magdalene. Before doing that, we must distinguish between the Mary's of the New Testament. Mary was a very common name for Jewish women during the first century and had its derivative from the name Miriam. There are at least seven distinct Mary's of the New Testament. We have Mary, the mother of Jesus, identified in the first chapter of Luke.[14] There is Mary, the mother of James (not the Lord's brother) and Joseph, identified in Matthew 27.[15] There is Mary, the wife of Clopas, found in John 19.[16] We also have Mary, the sister of Lazarus and Martha, identified in both Luke and John.[17] There is Mary, the mother of John Mark, identified in Acts 12.[18] There is an unidentified Mary whom we read about in Romans 16.[19] Finally there is Mary Magdalene, whom we will identify in depth in a few moments. These are all distinct Mary's, identified usually by the association with a male counterpart, either their husband or their sons, which was a reflection of the patriarchal first-century culture. Mary Magdalene, on the other hand, is not connected to a male name, and this could indicate that she may not have been married. Instead, Mary is identified as Mary Magdalene, which indicates the place of her origin, that of Magdala, a city southwest of Galilee alluded to in Matthew 15.[20]

Unfortunately, Mary Magdalene has been confused with other women of the New Testament. In 591 AD, Pope Gregory the Great, in his Easter sermon, identified the sinful woman in Luke 7 as Mary Magdalene. This is rather unfortunate, because there is no compelling reason to make this association. This has given rise to the idea that Mary Magdalene was a prostitute. We see this depicted in several movies, such as *The Last Temptation of Christ* by Martin Scorsese, as well as the 1960s Andrew Lloyd Webber musical, *Jesus Christ Superstar*.

The radical feminists, such as Lynn Picknett and Margaret Starbird, also connect Mary Magdalene to the Mary of John 12, and to the woman in Matthew 26 who anointed Jesus with precious ointment contained in an alabaster vessel. The reason for this connection is obvious when you understand the agenda of their absurd hypothesis. For the individual of Matthew 26 to be performing a sacred pagan rite of *hieros gamos*, and, therefore, a sexual marital rite, she would have to be Mary Magdalene, since, in their view, Christ and Mary Magdalene were devout lovers.

Lynn Picknett also says that there is no reason to believe that Mary came from the city of Magdala in Galilee; she even denies there was such a city. In fact, she says there are "compelling reasons to say she came from elsewhere." She claims that Mary could have hailed from Magdolum in Egypt or even Magdala in Ethiopia. This helps Ms. Picknett's case in trying to identify Mary Magdalene as the "priestess from Egypt."[21]

Margaret Starbird believes that Micah 4:8 refers to a prophecy concerning Mary Magdalene. The passage reads, "As for you, tower of the flock, heel of the daughter of Zion, to you it will come. Even the former dominion will come, the kingdom of the daughter of Jerusalem." Ms. Starbird makes this connection between Mary Magdalene and this verse by pointing out that the "tower" in verse 8 comes from the Hebrew word *migdal-eder*. In fact, this passage is actually alluding to the future captivity of Jerusalem by the Babylonian empire and the eventual redemption by the Lord from Babylonian captivity as evidenced in Micah 4:9-10.

Ms. Starbird goes on to say in her book, *The Woman with the Alabaster Jar,* that she suspects that "the epithet Magdalene" was meant to be an allusion to the Magdaleder (found in Micah), the promise of the restoration of Zion following her exile. She believes that the epithet "Magdalene," then, refers to these lines in Micah and has nothing to do with a town in Galilee. Furthermore, Ms. Starbird writes that since the word *Magdala* means "tower" or "elevated great magnificence," Mary's name would be the equivalent of "Mary the Great," and would have particular significance if Mary indeed was married to Jesus Christ.[22] As a consequence to this, Margaret Starbird has now given the title to Mary as "Goddess of the Gospels," thus the title of her book, *The Goddess and the Gospels: Reclaiming the Sacred Feminine.*

The fact is that the woman who anoints Jesus in Matthew 12, Mark 14, and John 12 is Mary of Bethany, the sister of Lazarus and Martha. Matthew's account does not identify the woman, but in John 12, Jesus had come to Bethany where Lazarus was, as well as Martha. In verse 3, Mary is identified as the woman who anointed Jesus.

Luke 10:38 identifies this Mary as the sister of Martha. Connecting Mary of Bethany to Mary Magdalene in this case is absurd, and constitutes an attempt to further one's own notions concerning Jesus and Mary Magdalene.

As stated earlier, some have confused the woman of Luke 7 who anointed Jesus' feet with Mary Magdalene, as well. Margaret Starbird and Lynn Picknett apparently believe this anointing is the same anointing performed by Mary of Bethany alluded to in the scriptures above. If one reads Luke 7 carefully, however, it is obvious that the woman anointing Jesus' feet in this passage is clearly not Mary Magdalene, nor is she Mary of Bethany. Her name is not given, but this anointing occurs at a different time chronologically than the anointing that occurred of Jesus by Mary of Bethany. In that anointing, Jesus' feet were anointed shortly before He was to be delivered up for crucifixion. The anointing in Luke 7 clearly occurs at an earlier time. The woman of Luke 7 is referred to as a "sinful woman" by the Pharisees. Indeed, her sins may have been sins of sexual impropriety. It is obvious from the Scriptures that she understood who Christ was and that Christ had the ability to forgive her sins—and He did so.

Mary Magdalene is introduced in chapter 8 of Luke and is clearly not identified with the woman of Luke chapter 7. She is introduced as a new character after Jesus had gone into another city. For this reason it is obvious that the woman in chapter 7 is not Mary Magdalene.

Before looking more closely at Mary Magdalene, a word should be said about the anointing of the feet of Christ that occurred in the Gospels. It has been proposed by Dan Brown and those liberal feminist theologians from whom he takes his ideas that Jesus' anointing was a premarital sexual right called *heiros gammos*. This is absurd.

The washing and anointing of the feet of Christ by the woman in Luke 7 and by Mary of Bethany in Matthew, Mark, and John, were acts of hospitality. It was not uncommon during the time of Jesus that when entering a house, to have one's feet washed and soothed with ointment. As was the custom of the day, people ambulated in sandals or bare feet. It would be an act of hospitality to offer a visitor the courtesy of washing and anointing the feet. These particular anointings were clearly important events, hence their recording in the Gospels. Their significance was showing the humility these women had toward Christ and in their acknowledgment of His true deity and purpose on earth.[23]

Let's turn now to what the Bible *does* say about Mary Magdalene. Mary Magdalene was certainly a devout follower of Christ, and along with many other women, was present at His death. She was a witness to His burial, and was the first person to see Christ after His resurrection. We are introduced to Mary Magdalene in Luke 8. That passage indicates that Christ had exorcised seven demons from Mary, and along with Joanna, the wife of Chuza, Herod's steward, and Susanna, and many others, she contributed to the support of Christ and His apostles from her private means. Mary Magdalene, along with Mary, mother of James and Joseph; Salome, the mother of the sons of Zebedi (James and John); Mary, the mother of Jesus; Mary, wife of Clopus; and other women were present at the crucifixion of Christ. Matthew 25 indicates that these women had ministered to Jesus and had followed Him from Galilee. Mary Magdalene also was a witness of Jesus' burial, along with Joseph of Arimathaea and Mary, the mother of James and Joseph. It was Mary Magdalene and "the other Mary" who also were the first to see the empty tomb.[24] Finally, John 20 says that Mary was the first to see Jesus after His resurrection. The apostle John stated in verse 13, "And they said to her, Woman, why are you weeping?" She said to them, "Because they have taken away my Lord and I do not know where they have laid him." And when she had said this, she turned around and beheld Jesus standing there and did not know that it was Jesus. Then Jesus said to her, "Woman, why are you weeping? Whom are you seeking?" Supposing him to be the gardener, she said to him, "Sir, if you have carried him away, tell me where you have laid him, and I will take him away." In verse 16, Jesus said to her, "Mary!" She turned and said to him in Hebrew, "Rabboni!" which means teacher. Then Jesus said to her, "Stop clinging to me for I have not yet ascended to the Father, but go to my brethren and say to them, I ascend to my Father and your Father and my God and your God." Afterward Mary Magdalene came announcing to the disciples, "I have seen the Lord."[25] This is the only point of time in the New Testament in which we see Jesus and Mary Magdalene alone, although Matthew 28 alludes to the same incident. This passage indicates that Mary, the mother of James and Joseph, may have been present at this time, too.[26]

In the entire New Testament, there are twelve passages that refer to Mary Magdalene. In summary, she was a disciple of Christ, and Jesus had cast seven demons out of her body. She ministered to Christ and supported Him and His apostles financially, along with many others. She was a witness to His crucifixion and a witness to His burial. She was the first to see Christ after His resurrection from the grave.[27] Finally, she had an important role in reporting to Christ's apostles concerning His resurrection. It is evident that she was devoted to Jesus and loved

Him, as evidenced in her reaction to Jesus at His resurrection. It is also obvious that Mary did not consider herself to be equal to Jesus. Matthew 28 indicates that she was worshipping Him after His resurrection.[28] It is also obvious the New Testament fails to mention or even hint that Jesus was married to Mary Magdalene or was her devout lover. It would seem painfully obvious that if this were the case, the New Testament would state so. Finally, it is also obvious that Jesus never stated that Mary was to be His "successor" on earth after His death. As we have already seen, Christ had no intention of having anyone other than Himself become the head of His Church, and certainly not Mary Magdalene. This in no way diminishes the important role that Mary Magdalene played in the life of Christ, nor that of the many other women mentioned in the New Testament.

Was Jesus the Original Feminist?

Dan Brown would have us believe Jesus was the original feminist.[29] By that, he tells us through his character Teabing, Jesus intended the future of His Church to be in the hands of Mary Magdalene. Furthermore, the character Robert Langdon tells us, "Constantine and his male successors successfully converted the world from matriarchal paganism to patriarchal Christianity by waging a campaign of propaganda that demonizes the sacred feminine, obliterating the goddess from the modern religion forever."[30] Both of these notions are absurd nonsense and could not be further from the truth. If, indeed, Constantine and his male successors wanted to wage war against women and thereby rewrite the New Testament, obliterating any positive references to women, as Dan Brown and his radical feminist theologians assert, then it would appear that they did a very poor job. What the New Testament does show is that Christianity had a liberating affect on women, and not vice versa.

First of all, there has never been a matriarchal society in the history of mankind. According to Steven Goldberg, Chairman of the Department of Sociology at City University of New York, fifty years of research has "failed to include a single shred of evidence that such matriarchies have ever existed, and demonstrated the inability of all such theories to deal with reality. Of the hundreds of societies that we have studied in this century, without exception, they have been patriarchal...."[31] Margaret Mead acknowledges, "It is true that all claims so glibly made about societies ruled by women are nonsense. We have no reason to believe they ever existed."[32] Furthermore, during Christ's time and before, women were treated with disdain and were little more than cattle or possessions. Pagan societies in Greece, India, and China gave women no rights at all, and women were considered as property to their husbands. Greek philosophers also did not esteem women. Aristotle taught that a woman ranked somewhere between a man and a slave. In ancient Greece, women had the social status of a slave, and it should be noted that this comes from the philosophy through which Gnosticism appeared. Plato, in his dialogue, *Timaes*, in espousing what later would become Gnostic theology stated that, "Anyone who lived well for his appointed time would return home to his native star and live an appropriately happy life; but anyone who failed to do so would be changed into a woman at his second birth."[33]

The Bible in both the Old and New Testaments actually deals very favorably with many women, and Christianity was liberating to women. Anyone who reads the Bible and comes to any other conclusions is not being honest with the text. To cite just a few examples from the Old Testament, look at Sarah, the wife of Abraham and the devotion and faith that she demonstrated.[34] We have the wisdom of Deborah, the judge and prophetess;[35]Jael, the wife of Heber, who showed tremendous bravery in the killing of the Canaanite commander, Sisera;[36] the bravery and faith of Rahab and her cunningness in the saving of the Hebrew spies at Jericho;[37] the loyalty of Ruth;[38] and the tremendous bravery and faith of Esther in dealing with Haman, the ruthless vassal of King Ahasuerus, the king of the Medopersian empire.[39]

In the New Testament, the importance of the female genealogy of Christ's birth is given in the first chapter of Matthew. We also see in the New Testament that Jesus freely discoursed with women during His ministry, including the Samaritan woman in John 4 when He first announced that He was the Messiah.[40] We have already seen that women, including Mary Magdalene, were part of the entourage who followed Jesus around and ministered to His needs. If the New Testament had been written by chauvinistic, women-hating men, why would they include these references? Repeatedly, throughout the New Testament, women are listed as disciples, helpers, teachers, and prophetesses. In Acts 16, Lydia was the first convert in Europe. In Romans 16, Phoebe was commended by Paul as a helper to many, including himself. Priscilla risked her life for Paul and was instrumental in the teaching of Apollo.[41] Paul also mentioned several other faithful servants, such as Mary and Julia.[42] Nympha, in Colossians 4, had a church in her house. Phillip had four daughters who were prophetesses.[43] Furthermore, I would also point out, once again, that a woman, Mary Magdalene, was the first to see Jesus risen from the grave. These are just some of the women mentioned in the New Testament who were important in the cause of Christ and Christianity. Finally, Paul stated in Galatians 3, "There is neither Jew nor Greek, there is neither slave nor freeman, there is neither male or female, for you all are one in Jesus Christ."[44] So, to say the New Testament writers were chauvinist women-haters is an absurdity.

This is not to say that women in the past may have been treated shabbily or persecuted by some in the name of Christianity or the Church. Mr. Brown points to the book *Malleus Maleficarum or The Witches' Hammer*. According to its author, many "free-thinking women were tortured and eventually killed." The authors claim that "over 300 years, an astounding five million women" were burned at the stake.[45] Robin Briggs of Oxford University challenges this number and states that in reality something between 40,000 and 50,000 executions occurred between the years 1450 and 1750, of which 20 to 25 percent were men.[46] Nonetheless, even one woman dying or being tortured by so-called Christians in this manner is too many. Having said that, because atrocities have occurred as a result of, or in the name of Christianity, does not prove or show that the *Bible* was responsible for this. It only demonstrates that there have been those that have distorted the *Bible* and abused their authority, or committed such heinous acts in the name of Christianity.

Was Jesus Married?

Briefly, the question has been put forth concerning the possibility of Christ having been married. On this the New Testament is silent. Surprisingly, it is the silence of the Scriptures that the authors of this concept offer as proof that He *was* married! Because the Scriptures do not state that Jesus was married, it is therefore assumed by them that He must have been. This seems strangely illogical to me. The theory goes that if Jesus was unmarried, the Bible would surely state such because of its significance.

It is further postulated that all Jewish men of Jesus' day were married, and it was virtually sinful for a man to remain single during this time in history. This is simply not true. Yes, most men were married in Christ's time, just as most adult men are married in our society. But it is not true that being unmarried was automatically viewed as sinful. There are multiple examples of unmarried men in the New Testament, the most obvious being the apostle Paul. Also, during the time of Christ, the Essenes existed. These were zealous Jews who are believed to be responsible for the copying of the Dead Sea Scrolls and the hiding of them in the caves of Qumran.[47] These people took vows of celibacy and were contemporaneous with Jesus Christ.

Proponents of this theory also site that because Jesus was a "rabbi" he would have been married. They state that all rabbis were married under Jewish law. This argument demonstrates ignorance of Jesus' linage and of Jewish law. Jesus was of the linage of David, hence the tribe of Judah. Traditionally, the Levites were "rabbis," or priests, under Jewish law, and Jesus was not a Levite![48] Jesus was a rabbi in the sense of being a teacher, which the word *rabbi* means, but He was clearly not a *Jewish rabbi* in the strictest sense of the word.

The more obvious question then becomes not, was Christ married, but whether He could have been married. Jewish law would not have prohibited this. Further, in the New Testament it is clear, Paul said marriage is "honorable and the marriage bed undefiled."[49] Jesus Himself ordained marriage in several passages of the New Testament.[50] So, clearly sexual union between husband and wife is not sinful, and if Jesus had chosen to be married, He would have committed no sin.

Having said that, I find it highly unlikely that Jesus was married. Contrary to some so-called experts, I find it very unreasonable to assume the silence of the Scriptures proves the marriage of Christ. It also seems very unlikely to me that Christ's mission on earth would have lent itself to marriage. Further, His knowledge concerning His persecution and eventual crucifixion and the pain this would cause a family would likely have dissuaded Him from marriage. In any event, speculation on this takes away from the true issue, which is the divinity of Christ. I believe those who put forth this doctrine are using it as a screen. What they are really getting at is the humanity of Christ. If they can get us to believe that Jesus was married, then the next step is believing that Jesus was just a man and not the Son of God, and therefore, not divine!

5

The Council of Nicea

Possibly the most egregious example of distortions
and exaggerations occuring in *The Da Vinci Code* concerns
its dealings with the Emperor Constantine and the Council of Nicea. Through the character Teabing, *The Da Vinci
Code* makes some rather outlandish suggestions concerning Constantine and the Council of Nicea that bear
examination. Teabing states that Constantine was baptized on his deathbed under protest, and was actually a
lifelong pagan. He further states that in order to unify
Rome under a growing "religious turmoil," Constantine
decided on Christianity as a national religion. He did this
because Constantine wished to "back the winning horse."
In doing this, he merged pagan symbols, rituals, and dates
into Christianity. Constantine shifted the worship of God
from Saturday to Sunday to coincide with the pagans'
"Veneration Day of the Sun."

In 325 AD, Constantine brought together over 300 bishops at the Council of Nicea. According to Teabing, the purpose of the Council of Nicea was to deify Jesus. Before the Council of Nicea, many Christians had considered Christ a powerful prophet and leader but only a man. Again according to character Teabing, it was important to establish Christ's divinity for the "further unification of the Roman Empire." Additionally, the character Teabing states, "many scholars claim that the early church literally stole Jesus from the original followers hijacking his human message, shrouding it in an impenetrable cloak of divinity and using it to expand their own power."[1] As a result in a "relatively close vote," the divinity of Jesus was established.

Also at the Council of Nicea, Constantine commissioned and financed a new Bible per *The Da Vinci Code*. Supposedly, this Bible was taken from more than "80 Gospels" that had been considered for the New Testament, but from which only a relatively few were chosen.[2] As a result, once again according to our character Teabing, gospels that spoke of Christ's human traits were omitted, and those gospels making him God-like were embellished and used to establish the New Testament as we have it today. These other "gospels" to which the character Teabing is referring are the Dead Sea Scrolls, which he says were found in 1950, and the Coptic scrolls of the Nag Hammadi, found in 1947. This, in fact, is not accurate. The Dead Sea Scrolls were discovered in 1947, and the Nag Hammadi writings, which are not scrolls at all, but codices, were found in 1945. In *The Da Vinci Code*, Teabing even characterizes the writings as "the earliest Christian records."[3] These texts were then ignored in order to accept writings that would more advance the political agenda of Constantine and promote "the divinity of the man Jesus Christ." As a result of this, possibly the most profound statement in *The Da Vinci Code* occurs when the character Teabing says, "Almost everything our fathers has taught us about Christ is false."[3] As a result, what Christians have held to be the modern Bible came from Constantine and has been the "truth for the ages,"[5] and other viable Gospels and Christian writings have been abandoned and destroyed.

So much for the fiction, now let's look at the facts. Constantine was the first "Christian" Roman emperor. He was born in 274 AD in what is now modern-day Albania, and he died on May 22, 337 AD. He was a soldier in the Roman army and fought under Diocletian in 296 in Egypt and then in the Persian war. At that time, Rome was divided into two empires, the east and the west. Constantine's father, Constantinus Chlorus, ruled in the west. After the death of his father, Constantine became emperor of the western empire of Rome. There was much division and turmoil in Rome at that time; eventually there would be six leaders of Rome, three in the west and three in the east. Through a series of fortunate events and hard-fought battles, eventually Constantine became sole emperor of the west. Between 323 and 324 AD, through several battles against Licinus, the emperor of the east, Constantine eventually became the sole emperor of the Roman Empire. As a result of this, Constantine moved the capital city to Byzantium, which he renamed Constantinople. It was in 312 AD that Constantine converted to Christianity, being the son of a practicing Christian. Constantine did defer his formal baptism until he was close to death, but this was a common practice during that time, and he was not baptized under protest.[6]

As far as the sincerity of Constantine's conversion, that is one for the historians to debate, but history does reveal that he did profess publicly his belief in one God and the divinity of Jesus Christ, although he continued to tolerate paganism.

As far as the idea of paganism and Christianity warring against each other during Constantine's time, there is no historical fact to support the notion as proposed by the character Teabing. In fact, if there was any war, it was in the form of religious persecution levied by the pagans at the Christians! At that time, Christians were in a distinct minority, making up no more than 5 to 8 percent of the entire population. After Constantine's conversion to Christianity, there is no doubt that Christianity proliferated in Rome. It became the popular religion, and multitudes began converting to Christianity during Constantine's reign. Constantine had given the Edict of Milan in 313, which allowed religious toleration throughout Rome and caused Christianity to flourish unfettered after three centuries of Roman persecution. In 325, Constantine called a council of bishops together at the city of Nicea to resolve a problem of unity within the Christian Church. This came to be referred to as the Council of Nicea. The Council of Nicea, however, was not convened to determine the divinity of Christ nor to rewrite the New Testament, as alleged by the character Teabing in *The Da Vinci Code*.[7] There has never been a dispute over the divinity of Christ since the inception of Christianity. The concept that early Christians did not consider Christ to be God is simply not based in any historical fact. The question debated at the Nicea Council was how to understand Jesus' divinity in light of His obvious human characteristics. In other words, how could

Jesus be both God and human, and yet there also be only one God? In the early fourth century, a man by the name of Arius from Alexandria, Egypt, held the concept that Christ was a divine being, but that He was subordinate to God the Father at His creation. This view made Christ subservient to God the Father and not fully God Himself.

A young deacon from the Alexandrian church, Athanasius, opposed this doctrine. He viewed Christ as being of the same essence as God the Father. This view would ultimately lead to the orthodox doctrine of the Trinity, which maintains that there are three persons who make up the one Godhead. The Council of Nicea met to decide this issue, and it was not a particularly close vote. In fact, only two of 300 bishops who met declined to sign the document that agreed with Athanasius's point of view; therefore, the only question at the Nicea Council was not whether Christ was divine, but *how* He was divine, and this was what the vote centered around.

Contrary to *The Da Vinci Code*, Constantine and the Council of Nicea did not meet to rewrite the history books nor to decide on the canon of the New Testament. Constantine actually had nothing to do with the formation of the canon as scripture. He did not choose books to include or exclude, and he did not order the destruction of other gospels. There were certainly no imperial book-burning ceremonies, as alluded to in *The Da Vinci Code*. Actually, much of what we know now as the canon of the New Testament was already accepted well before the time of Constantine. Christians had already been accepting some books as canonical and refusing others hundreds of years before the Council of Nicea.

What may have confused Teabing (or Dan Brown) is that Eusabius tells us in his biography, *The Life of Constantine*, written in the year 331, Constantine did commission fifty manuscripts of the Christian Bible to be copied by Eusabius for his churches throughout Constantinople. This commission did not involve a decision on Constantine's part in choosing which of the gospels were to be included or excluded. There is no evidence that Constantine had any concern as to the content of these Bibles.

The Council of Nicea was also convened to summarize the articles of basic Christian belief. Led by Athanasius, the Nicean Creed was produced. The Nicean Creed reads as follows:

We believe in one God, the Father of Almighty, Maker of all things both visible and invisible; and in one Lord Jesus Christ, the Son of God, the begotten of the Father, only the begotten, that is of one substance with the Father; by whom all things both in heaven and earth were made; who for us men and our salvation came down and was incarnate, became man, suffered and rose again the third day; ascended into the heavens; cometh to judge the quick and the dead; and in the Holy Spirit.

How Did We Get the New Testament?

At this point something must be said about how we obtained the New Testament that exists today. On this point, *The Da Vinci Code* has it right. The gospels of Christ and the New Testament did not come down from heaven on a fax machine, nor were they dictated on tablets of brass by an angel of heaven and recorded by man.[8] In fact, the New Testament, much like the Old Testament, was written by several different authors and came into being over a long period of time. It is evident that the core of the New Testament, the four gospels and the thirteen letters of Paul, were accepted as early as 130 AD as canon.[9] The four gospels—Matthew, Mark, Luke, and John—were written as eyewitness accounts of the life of Christ. It is obvious from the works of second-century theologians like Irenaeus and third-century theologians like Tertullian that the four gospels were affirmed to be original and part of what would become the canon of the gospels. The book of Acts was an eyewitness account written by the physician, Luke, of the things that transpired during the early days of Christianity and the establishment of Christianity, particularly the life and the missions of Paul. The epistles were primarily written by the apostles to churches throughout Judea and Asia and were inspired by the Holy Spirit to contain the doctrines of Christianity. They were read and circulated throughout all of the churches. Justin Martyr, an acquaintance of the apostle Paul, writing in the second century, referred to the gospels as, "The Memories, which I saw were drawn up by his Apostles and those who followed them."[10] All of the books of the New Testament were thus written between 50 and 120 AD.

Christians then would be anxious to have the New Testament documents placed in a canon, but this was obviously not accomplished during that period of time. Paul alluded to this in his letter to the Corinthians, in which he stated, "For we know in part and prophesy in part but when the perfect comes, the partial will be done away."[11] Until that time, Christians were to circulate the letters written by the apostles and read them to each other. Paul requested the Colossians to circulate the letter he had written to them to the church of Laodicea and vice versa.[12] Also Peter refers to Paul's writings as scripture in his epistle, also indicating that Paul's letters were being circulated throughout the Christian churches at the time.[13]

The early Christians were used to a canon of scriptures, especially those of Jewish heritage, and would be seeking to develop those scriptures. Paul told Timothy to handle accurately "the word of truth."[13] The other religions of the day were not as rooted in sacred text as Judaism and eventually Christianity. There were no writings that were used by these religions as guideposts as to what to believe and how to behave.

It should not be surprising during the New Testament time to have other writings emerge that would contain messages not found in the epistles and gospels. Early Christian leaders such as Eusebius, Ignatius, and Justin Martyr recognized these writings as heretical and sought to canonize the New Testament in order to have a unified doctrine. For writings to be included as canon four criteria were used. First, the writing had to be ancient and date back to nearly the time of Jesus. Next, the writings would have to be apostolic, that is, either written by one of the apostles or a companion to the apostles, such as the gospel of Luke and the book of Acts. Forgeries written in the name of Paul by other men, such as the Marcionites, would be rejected. Third, the book had to be catholic, that is, have widespread acceptance among the established churches at the time. The word *catholic* here means "universal" and does not refer to what is now known as the Catholic Church. Finally, and by far the most important criteria would be the orthodoxy of the scripture. This had to do with the nature of the view set forth in the book. In other words, it had to conform to the doctrines contained in the other accepted books. This would be a reason for disputing the Gnostic writings and not including them in the canon of the New Testament, as they contained dogma and doctrine that were foreign to the other works. It should be noted also that the writings and teachings of the apostles were accompanied by miracles to confirm that their word was indeed from God.[15]

In conclusion, Constantine was indeed one of the most important figures in early Christianity, advancing Christianity throughout the world. His conversion marks one of the greatest events in Christian history. He did not, however, decide on the divinity of Christ, and he did not decide on the canon of the New Testament. Developing the canon of the New Testament was a process that took several centuries. Although much of the canon was already in place by the middle of the second century, it was not until 367 AD, when Athanasius included, among his advice, a list of books that he felt appropriate to be read in the church. This list contained the twenty-seven books that we have now as our modern-day New Testament. Although some debates continued for centuries, eventually these twenty-seven books became accepted throughout the Christian world as the canon of New Testament scripture.

Did Constantine shift Christian worship from Saturday to Sunday?

According to *The Da Vinci Code*, Constantine shifted Christian worship from the Jewish Sabbath to Sunday to "coincide with the Pagan's veneration of the Sun." According to the character Robert Langdon, "To this day, most church goers attend services on Sunday morning with no idea that they are there on account of the Pagan Sun God's weekly tribute—Sunday."[16] This is just another one of the great untruths in *The Da Vinci Code*. Constantine certainly did not initiate Sunday worship services, as Christians were worshiping God on Sunday from the very beginning of Christianity.

The proof of this is foremost found in the New Testament itself. In Acts 20:7, Luke stated that Christians met on the first day of the week. Paul instructed in 1 Corinthians 16:2 that on the first day of the week they were to lay by him in store or put aside, as they might prosper, that no collections would be made when he would come. This obviously implies that the Christians were coming together on the first day of the week. Finally, in Revelation 1:10, John referred most likely to the first day of the week as "The Lord's Day." Why would Christians change worship from the Sabbath to the Lord's Day? Obviously, it was on the first day of the week that Christ was resurrected from the dead. Also, from Acts 20:7 we can see that the Christians partook of the Lord's Supper in commemoration of the death, burial, and resurrection of Jesus Christ. If the New Testament was all we had to prove that Christians met on the first day of the week prior to 325 AD, that would be enough. However, there are other proofs that corroborate that early Christians met on the first day of the week.

The tradition of the early Church chronicled by the so-called early church fathers, among them Ignatius of Antioch and Justin Martyr, clearly indicate that Christians were meeting on the first day of the week centuries prior to the birth of Constantine. Justin Martyr, who lived between 100 and 165 AD, wrote, "And on the day called

Sunday, there is a gathering together to one place of all those who live in cities or in the country, and the memoirs of the Apostles or the writings of the prophets are read, as long as time permits; then when the reader has ceased, the president presents admonition and invitation to the imitation of these good things."[17]

Even the testimonies of a pagan indicate that Christians met on the first day of the week. Pliny the Younger, in writing to the emperor Tragan, in the early second century, stated that Christians came together on a "fixed day" to "chant verses alternately amongst themselves in honor of Christ as if to a God." The fixed day to which Pliny was referring was Sunday.[18] These are but a few examples of numerous writings of antiquity indicating that Christians met on the first day of the week long before the time of Constantine.

So, clearly Mr. Brown distorts the truth in claiming that Constantine shifted the day of worship from the Sabbath to the first day of the week. This is not to say that Constantine may have tried to incorporate some pagan ideas into Christianity, but clearly Christians were worshiping God on the first day of the week from the very beginning.

6
Gnosticism

According to Dan Brown, the discovery of the Gnostic writings at the Nag Hammadi in Egypt in 1945 was one of the greatest discoveries of the twentieth century. In his mind, it rivals the discovery of the Dead Sea Scrolls, which were found in the Judean desert of Qumran in 1947. According to Dan Brown, the Gnostic writings tell the "original history of Christ," alleging that New Testament history is erroneous and tainted. He states that the Gnostic works were original Christian texts "highlighting glaring historic discrepancies and fabrications clearly confirming that the modern Bible was compiled and edited by men who possessed a political agenda—to promote the divinity of the man Jesus Christ and use his influence to solidify their own power base."[1]

One would gather from Mr. Brown's book that the Gnostic scriptures were written contemporaneously with the New Testament and were as much inspired as the New

Testament writings. Mr. Brown would also have us believe the "80 Gospels" were considered for the New Testament all at one time. First of all, there are no eighty Gnostic writings, and they are not "gospels," as we shall see in this chapter. Further in this chapter we will look extensively at Gnosticism, the theology and cosmology behind Gnosticism, the validity of Gnostic writings, and how they compare with the New Testament. Let us now look closely at the so-called Gnostic gospels and see what the truth is, since these "false gospels" are a large part of Mr. Brown's story. Additionally, because Mr. Brown alludes to the *Gnostic Gospels* by Elaine Pagels and apparently takes a lot of his information from that book, we will examine it throughout this chapter and more at the end in detail.

First and foremost, the Gnostic gospels are not "gospels" at all, and they are certainly not the earliest Christian records.[2] Even Ms. Pagels at this time is backing off calling these scriptures "gospels." Also, many of the parchments or codices found at Nag Hammadi are not Christian, and Christian features are completely absent from them. For example, Plato's *Republic* was found in the Nag discovery, and two of the Gnostic writings are Hermetic or Egyptian. Further the Nag Hammadi scriptures do not contain all the Gnostic writings that are extant. Knowledge of Gnosticism and Gnostic writings has been unearthed since 1769, although it is true that the bulk of the Gnostic writings come from the Nag Hammadi codices.[3] These codices were probably copies of original writings written in Greek, and not Aramaic, as Mr. Brown writes.

"Gnostic scriptures" were never considered orthodox scriptures, for reasons we will see later. First, though, I would encourage readers to examine the Gnostic writings and judge for themselves. From a literary perspective, they do not compare with the New Testament. Most of them are rambling, and they are not in a narrative form as the New Testament scriptures are. They can be very difficult to read, especially if one is not familiar with Gnostic doctrine and Gnostic jargon. An example of this comes from the "First Thought in Three Persons" taken from the Nag Hammadi. In talking about Barbéló in the first chapter, the verse reads, "I am invisible within the thinking of the invisible. I am disclosed within the immeasurable ineffable. I am incomprehensible, existing within the incomprehensible and moving within every creature. It is I who am the life of my afterthought." Also, in that same work, in describing the creation of the universe, the text reads, "and the great demon began to order eternal realms (aeons) in the manner of the eternal realms that exist. And it ordered them only because of its power." These "scriptures" are somewhat typical of Gnostic writings, and as one can see, difficult to interpret if one is unfamiliar with the nomenclature and the theology. In many cases one could call the writings bizarre. Also, virtually all the Gnostic writings contain references to the Old Testament and most contain direct quotes from the New Testament, especially those writings found at the Nag Hammadi. For this reason, it is clear these writings postdated New Testament and Old Testament scripture.

The authors of the Gnostic scriptures, again especially those of the Nag Hammadi, are difficult to discern. They are written in *pseudepigraphia*, works attributed to an authoritarian ancient figure such as Adam, Seth, or John the Apostle, but not actually written by them. This is a distinct difference from the New Testament in which the authors of the New Testament were men who were "eye-witnesses to the events they wrote about."[4]

When reading Gnostic literature, the observer must also keep in mind there is a very complex and distinctive myth of the origins of the universe, and once again, a very special language or jargon used in describing this myth. Otherwise, it would make no sense at all. Also, much is clearly "borrowed" from the Old Testament.

It is somewhat difficult to characterize completely Gnostic scriptures and theology, but an attempt will be made. Before looking into that, however, one cannot deny that Gnosticism made up a sect of Christianity in the second and third centuries. Valentinus was a prominent Gnostic in the second century, and some of the writings found in the Nag Hammadi are attributed to him or his followers. A church "father," Irenaus, writing in 180 AD, refuted Gnosticism in his great work *Against Heresies*. The question then becomes, when did Gnosticism begin and where did it have its origins? There is evidence that almost certainly Gnosticism existed centuries before the birth of Christ, although no one can give a precise date when it began.

Clearly Plato espoused a belief in his dialogue *Timeas* that is Gnostic in its theology. Gnosticism in the first and second centuries may have been a form of neo-Platonism. The word *Gnostic* means "knowledge," and to the Gnostic, salvation came by obtaining "gnosis" or true knowledge or enlightenment or acquaintance. Plato stated in *Timeas*: "But a man who has given his heart to learning and true wisdom and exercised that part of himself is surely found if he attains to the truth and to have immortal and divine thoughts, and cannot fail to achieve immortality as fully as permitted to human nature."[5] Further, Plato delineated the ancient Greek myth of the origins of the universe that are part of the Gnostic myth. (Keep in mind Plato also spoke of the Atlantis myth as well!) Finally, in Plato's *Timeas*, the author wrote about reincarnation, which is also a part of Gnostic theology. Plato wrote that men who "lived cowardly or immoral lives were reborn in the second generation as women."[6] Plato wrote this about 350 years before Christ. So, clearly from Plato's writings, it is evident that Gnosticism existed well before the age of the New Testament. With these thoughts in mind, let us look more closely at Gnosticism and its literature.

Gnostic Theology and Cosmology

Before going into any great detail about Gnosticism, it must first be realized that Gnosticism is a very complex theology with varying accounts of the Gnostic myth, showing wide variation in details. It is also apparent that Gnosticism has a very "eastern flavor," and there are some who believe that Gnosticism had its origins in Eastern Mysticism. Edward Consey, a British scholar of Buddhism, suggests this when he points out that Buddhists were in contact with the "Thomas Christians" in South India. Trade routes between the Far East and Rome were opening up at the time Gnosticism began to flourish in the late first and early second centuries. It is also noted that Hippolytus, a Christian in Rome around 225 AD, knew of the Indian Brahmins. So, when one examines the theology of Gnosticism, one can see a very eastern flavor with Hindu and Buddist connotations.[7]

In the Gnostic myth, the term *first principle* is used to describe a perfect, omnipotent, and ultimate divine source. For some inexplicable reason, this first principle emits a "hypostasis or second being and subsequently other beings or emanations." These emanations are called "aeons, or in Greek *aiones*," (*aeons* means "realms," "ages"), entities, and eternal realms and can at one time be places, periods of time (extracts of time), and even abstractions and are referred to by such names as "forethought," "eternal life," and "incorruptibility." The last *aeon* emitted was wisdom, or "Sophia." Nowhere in Gnostic literature is the question addressed of why the first principle would create these lesser, imperfect "second principles."

The first principle, then, is a solitary intellect that functions only to think, with the only object of its thought being itself. This act of thinking becomes objectified in the second principle. This "solitary eye" of the first principle functions then solely to look at itself, and its reflection then is the second principle. The first principle is a "spring of water that overflows into the second principle." *Barbéló*, or *Barbéró*, is the name given to the second principle. This character is seen in various versions of the Gnostic myth. Other characters in the Gnostic myth include the "four luminaries:" *Harmozél*, *Óroiaél*, *Dauethia*, and *Elébíth*, who are *aeons* and therefore eternal realms and actors. In neo-Plato-Gnosticism, "Christ," or the anointed, is also a metaphysical aeon that some versions have descending to unite with the man Jesus of Nazareth. In the Gnostic theology, Christ and Jesus are then two separate entities. Gnostics have Jesus dying on the cross, but not Christ. This concept is known as docetism. Getting back to the four luminaries, they are viewed as dwelling places, and they are the realms of the four archetypes—*Geradamas* or *Adamas*, the heavenly Adam; Seth, the heavenly prototype of Adam's son; the heavenly posterity of Seth, who are the prototypes of the Gnostic church on earth; and a fourth group whose identity varies throughout the Gnostic myth.

After the spiritual universe has been completely emitted, there then became a need for a "craftsman" to be created who would then create the world. His name is given *Ialdabaóth* and is clearly modeled after Plato's myth found in *Timeas*. Ialdabaóth equates with the Hebrew Jehovah in the Gnostic theology and is a bad, or evil, character. He is viewed as arrogant, selfish, and desirous of the divine even to the point of lusting for it, even raping for it. This being, that is Ialdabaóth, is responsible for creating material aeons, "realms," such as the stars, the planets, and the heavenly spheres. His offspring would be "powers," "demons," "angels," "authorities," etc. Because Ialdabaóth and his heavenly "rulers" attempt to dominate all human affairs, sexual lust is created, and humanity then is enslaved to them. As to why Ialdabaóth is so imperfect is only speculation within the Gnostic myth, but in some versions he is the son of Sophia, Wisdom, the result of a previous lustful act on her part.

It should be emphasized that the god of the Gnostics is the first principle and is not identified with the god of Israel, the creator of the cosmos. Instead, the god of Israel is equated with Ialdabaóth, the "imperfect craftsman," or *Sabaoth*, his firstborn, depending upon which version of the Gnostic myth you choose to accept. In essence, in the Gnostic myth, the god of Israel is equated with Saklar, or Satan. It is through wisdom's (Sophia's) effort to regain the power stolen by Ialdabaóth that Adam and the human race is created. In fact, it is through sexual intercourse between Sophia and Ialdabaóth that Adam is actually created. From this point, the plot closely resembles the first four chapters in Genesis, but with the obvious change to make the actions of the creator imperfect. The firstborn of Adam is Seth, and it is through Seth that the Gnostics believe their origins emanated. The Gnostics believe that Seth possessed true "acquaintance," and through him sprang a great race of people who are now the enlightened ones, also called the Gnostics. Eve's first two sons, Cain and Abel, were not the product between her and Adam according to the Gnostic myth, but they were rather a result of Ialdabaóth raping Eve. The Gnostics believe that Adam, Seth, and Eve were created of the heavenly spheres and then were incarnated into a fleshly body on earth.

For Gnostics, we are in the final days of their myth. The Savior, or Christ, was sent in order to "awaken" mankind to allow them to acquire "gnosis," or acquaintance. When this occurs, it frees the soul from the bonds of humanity and materiality and allows the soul to escape reincarnation. Those who do not accept *gnosis* are thus reincarnated in some form on the earth. As can be seen, this closely resembles the Hindu and Buddhist religions. There is, however, a "greater punishment" reserved for the apostate Gnostics that is not truly spelled out in the Gnostic myth.[8] What happens at the end of time varies among Gnostic writings, but most have a final destruction occurring to the "craftsman" and the evil rulers of the Earth.

What is very vague in Gnostic literature is defining exactly what *gnosis*, or *acquaintance*, is. Is it accepting the Gnostic theology and cosmology? Or is it some other higher order or insight into one's being? Furthermore, it is not detailed as to how one actually achieves this gnosis or acquaintance.

Jesus' role in the Gnostic myth is that of the pre-existing Christ, who is also referred to as the Word, the pre-existent Seth, or *Barbéló*. As stated earlier, Gnostics believe in the doctrine of docetism, which is that the real Jesus did not exist in human flesh but only appeared to do so; therefore His death on the cross was not real. The Gnostics do not accept the idea of Christ leading a material life and dying for the sins of the world.

From this very brief discussion of Gnosticism, it is easy to see why first-century Christians rejected it. It is clear from the New Testament writings that Jesus and His apostles accepted the Greek Septuagint version of the Old Testament as inspired. For that reason alone, the teachings of the Gnostics would be abominable to them. To consider the God of Israel as an "evil craftsman" or demiurge by first-century Jews and first-century Christians would be blasphemous.

Although not expressly stated, I do believe that the epistles of John deal specifically with Gnostism. In chapter 2 of his first epistle, John warned of a spirit of anti-Christ that was coming that would come from "out of us."[9] The antichrist would deny the Father and deny the deity of Jesus Christ. The antichrist would not believe that Jesus came in the flesh.[10] John called this a spirit of error. John 4:6 warns Christians to "test" the spirits to see whether they are from God, because many false prophets have gone out into the world.[11] John stated in John 4:4: "And we have beheld and bear witness that the Father has sent the Son to be the Savior of the world. Whoever confesses that Jesus is the Son of God, God abides in him and he in God." Again in 2 John 7, the apostle wrote that the one who does not acknowledge that Jesus has come in the flesh is the deceiver and the antichrist. Finally, John stated that it is through a love of God and the keeping of His commandments that we show our love for Him.[12] It is also likely that Hymenaeus and Philetus, mentioned in 2 Timothy 2, were Gnostics. Their view that the resurrection had already taken place is advocated in the Gnostic books, *The Treaties on Resurrection, The Exegesis on the Soul,* and *The Gospel of Phillip* found in The Nag Hammadi Library.[13]

I believe that the early Gnostics borrowed from Christianity and placed Christ, the anointed one, into their theology just as a modern Hindu or Buddhist might try to do. One cannot believe in the deity of Christ as taught in the New Testament and accept Gnosticism; they are mutually exclusive.

Gnostic Writings

I would now like to look at some specific Gnostic texts, or "scriptures," especially those found at the Nag Hammadi. As mentioned earlier, the Nag Hammadi codices, as they are called, were discovered by an Egyptian peasant in 1945. They were buried at Nag Hammadi in sealed pots by unknown persons centuries ago. They are not scrolls as Mr. Brown states in *The Da Vinci Code*, but rather books or codices written on various materials, predominantly papyrus. It has been said that it is primarily an accident of geography and climate that these texts exist at all today. How the Nag discoveries came to light and eventually result in the codices residing in the Coptic Museum in Cairo is a story of mystery, intrigue, and scholastic envy. Eventually, however, the Nag Hammadi writings became available for scholastic study and interpretation and were translated into English. They were published in 1977 in the original Nag Hammadi Library, edited by James M. Robinson.[14]

The Gnostic writings of the Nag Hammadi are contained in some twelve codices plus eight leaves from a thirteenth. They contain fifty-two separate tractates. Since there is duplication of some of these tractates, there are actually forty-five separate titles. The Nag Hammadi writings were written in Coptic, an ancient Egyptian language. Scholars believe these Coptic texts were copies of much earlier original works written in Greek. The date of copying probably occurred around 350 AD, although no exact date can be given. The date of the original Greek manuscripts is even more difficult to pinpoint precisely, but most scholars believe the original works were written in the second and mid-third centuries. Because of the variation in the codices' size, handwriting, writing materials, and dialects, it is felt that the codices were collected from various places along the Nile and placed at the Nag Hammadi.

The exact authorship of each tractate in the *Nag Hammadi Library* is unknown, as most, if not all, of the codices are examples of pseudepigraphia—meaning the alleged author of the work is not the actual author but has "borrowed" the name. For example, *The Secret Book according to John* was not written by John the apostle but by some unknown person using John's name, hence *pseudepigraphia*. (By the way, that book actually begins "Once upon a time"!)

Some of the Nag tractates were written by followers of Valentinus, a prominent Gnostic of the second century, born in Egypt and eventually residing in Rome, where he had a dominant influence. The oft-cited and much-studied *Gospel of Phillip* and *Gospel of Thomas*, also examples of pseudepigraphia, came from the Valentinus school. We will look at these two works, as well as the *Gospel of Mary*. This work is not found in the Nag Hammadi Library, but is an ancient Gnostic writing that was discovered in 1896 and is part of the *Papyrus Berolinesis* now residing in Berlin. It is these three Gnostic writings to which Dan Brown alludes in *The Da Vinci Code*, as does Elaine Pagels in her book, *The Gnostic Gospels*.

It should be considered that many of the Nag Hammadi tractates contain nothing Christian at all, but simply tell the Gnostic myth. Where Christ is found in the Nag scriptures, He comes across with a very Gnostic slant. It is true that much of our information concerning the Gnostics has come from the Nag Hammadi, but Gnosticism was well-known before the discovery at the Nag in 1945, as some five codices containing fourteen works were extant before that time.[15] Even without these Gnostic codices, the polemic works of Irenaeus, in particular his *Treaties against Heresies*, gives a very accurate picture of the Gnostic theology and cosmology as confirmed by the Nag codices.

We shall now look at *The Gospel of Phillip*, *The Gospel of Thomas*, and *The Gospel of Mary* in particular, because it is these Gnostic writings that contain references to Mary Magdalene, which are part of *The Da Vinci Code* story. It should be emphasized, however, if one examines the Gnostic writings to find input concerning Mary Magdalene, one will become very disappointed, as there is actually very little reference to Mary Magdalene in the entirety of the Gnostic scriptures.

The Gospel of Phillip

The Gospel of Phillip sets forth the idea that Jesus and Mary Magdalene were companions, and hence, husband and wife, according to modern-day feminist theologians. *The Gospel of Phillip* states: "And the companion of [...Mary Magdalene.] The [...loved] her more than [all the disciples,] [and he used to] [kiss her on] [...more] often than the rest of his disciples."[16] Modern theologians have to fill in the brackets because they are missing in the Coptic text. Therefore, modern theologians would fill in the brackets to say "...and the companion of the Savior was Mary Magdalene. The Savior or Christ loved her more than all the disciples and used to kiss her on the mouth more often than the rest of the disciples." That is a lot of filling in the blanks! The feminist theologians also refer to, as does Dan Brown, section 28 of *The Gospel of Phillip*, which states, "Three women always used to walk with the Lord, Mary, his mother, his sister, and the Magdalene who is also called his companion. For Mary is the name of his sister and his mother and it is the name of his partner."[17] From this, the modernists say that Jesus and Mary were husband and wife! Keep in mind, however, this comes from the same work that says that "God is a cannibal"[18] and that "human beings are supreme over animals from some hidden faculty and for this reason they dominate animals that are stronger than they and larger in external appearance in hidden capacity!"[19] With these thoughts in mind, let us briefly look at the *Gospel of Phillip*.

The *Gospel of Phillip* is a Valentinian anthology. It actually contains some one hundred short exerpts from a variety of works. These works include sermons, treaties, or philosophical epistles.[20] Both the compiler and the original writers of these works are completely unknown at this time, and certainly the term *gospel* should not be mistaken for the gospels of the New Testament since it bears no resemblance to the New Testament gospels in either literary form or inspiration. The *Gospel of Phillip* is not a narrative and certainly does not detail the life of Christ or His teachings. In fact, the reason for the title may be that Phillip is the only apostle mentioned in the anthology.[21] Like all of the Nag Hammadi writings, it is in Coptic, translated in around 350 AD or just before, with its original Greek not surviving.

The key significance to the *Gospel of Phillip* for our study has already been mentioned. To give a better flavor to this "gospel," I would like to refer to a few verses. Admittedly, some of this is nonsensical. For example, in plate 2 verse 13, "if a dead person inherits the living, that person will not die but rather will greatly live."[22] In section 3 verse 15: "A gentile does not die, for the gentile has never become alive so as to die. One who has believed in the truth has become alive and this person runs the risk of dying because of being alive." This is the sort of nonsensical verbiage that Mr. Brown would have us believing is comparable to New Testament writings! In section 6: "Light and darkness, life and death, right and left, are siblings (that is mutually dependent); it is impossible for them to separate."[23] In section 14: "Some said that Mary conceived by the Holy Spirit; they are mistaken, they do not realize what they say, when did a female ever conceive by a female?"[24] In section 17, the *Gospel of Phillip* puts forth the concept that Gnostics had regarding Christ and Jesus: "Jesus is a private name, Christ 'anointed' is a public name therefore Jesus does not exist (as a word) in any language but rather his name by which he is called is Jesus. But the word for Christ in Syriac is Messias, and in the Greek Khristos, and probably all the others have it according to the particular language of each. The Nazarene is the public name of the private name."[25] Not to belabor the point, but more absurdities occur in section 19, which reads: "Those who say that the Lord first died and then rose are mistaken, for he arose and then died. If one does not first get resurrection one will not die."[26] There is much of this Gnostic dribble throughout the *Gospel of Phillip*.

For those who say the *Gospel of Phillip* was contemporaneous with New Testament writings, it would seem hard to explain how thirteen direct quotes from the New Testament occur in it. Two excellent examples of this occur in section 64: "My God, my God, why O' Lord has thou forsaken me,"[27] which is a direct quote from Mark 15:34, as well as section 21: "Flesh and blood will not inherit the Kingdom of God,"[28] a direct quote from 1 Corinthians 15:50. So, clearly, the compilers of the *Gospel of Phillip* had New Testament writings before them when putting this work together.

The Gospel of Thomas

The *Gospel of Thomas* is an anthology of supposed "obscure" sayings of Jesus. Allegedly these were collected and transmitted by Didymous Jude Thomas. This again is an example of pseudepigraphy, as certainly Jude Thomas did not compile these sayings. Again, it is not in a narrative form, but rather rambling sayings attributed to Christ. Its importance to *The Da Vinci Code* occurs in the last section, with its reference to Mary, which is assumed to be referencing Mary Magdalene. Simon Peter said: "Mary should leave us, for females are not worthy of life." Jesus said: "See I'm going to attract her to make her male so that she too might become a living spirit that resembles you males. For every female element that makes itself male will enter the Kingdom of Heaven."[29] Curiously, Elaine Pagels refers to this statement in the *Gospel of Thomas* as "puzzling." I would say the only reason it is puzzling is because it does not fit into her feminist agenda. How can we have the Gnostics who were supposed to be early feminists and pro-women making such a statement in their scriptures?[30]

A closer look at the *Gospel of Thomas* reveals that New Testament Scriptures are quoted 166 times in this work. Again this indicates that the *Gospel of Thomas* was compiled after the New Testament Scriptures had been in circulation.

The *Gospel of Thomas* exists in its full form in a single Coptic translation from the Nag Hammadi. There are, however, fragments of the *Gospel of Thomas* that are written in Greek that reside in the Oxford London and Cambridge Libraries. These Greek manuscripts contain only small portions of the text. The original Greek work was written before 200 AD but after the advent of Christianity and most certainly after the gospels of Matthew, Mark, and Luke.[31] Some have attributed the writing of the *Gospel of Thomas* to the "Q" document, the supposed last record of Jesus' sayings in His own handwriting. Of course, there is no evidence of such a "Q" document, although Mr. Brown alludes to such in his book.

Just as *The Gospel of Phillip* is not in the narrative form, neither is the *Gospel of Thomas*, and again, the word *gospel* should not be mistaken for the literary form of the gospels in the New Testament. The *Gospel of Thomas* is rambling, alleged sayings of Christ that form no continuity of thought or particular order.

Gnosticism

An example of some of the non-New Testament sayings occurs in the *Gospel of Thomas*, in section 7: "Jesus
said, 'Blessed is the lion that the human will devour so
that the lion becomes human, and cursed the human being that the lion devours; and the lion will become
human.'"[32] Another supposed quote from Jesus in section
15 reads: "When you see one who has not been born of
woman, fall upon your faces and prostrate yourself before that one; it is that one who is your father."[33] Also, in
section 49, Jesus said: "Blessed are those who are solitary and superior for you will find the kingdom; for since
you come from it you shall return to it."[34] And finally, an
especially and obscure and somewhat silly quotation in
section 42: "Be passer by."[35] One could quote many more
of these supposed sayings of Jesus, but these suffice to
give the flavor of the Gnostic *Gospel of Thomas*.

An example of how the Gnostics try to incorporate
Christ into their theology can be seen in section 67, in
which Jesus said, "If anyone should be acquainted with
the entirety and should fall short of all that person falls
short utterly."[36] In section 86, the Gnostics twist Matthew 8:20 and Luke 9:58 to fit their theology: "Foxes have
their dens and birds have their nests but the son of man
has no where to lay his head and gain repose."[37]

As mentioned previously, many New Testament quotations occur in the *Gospel of Thomas*. What is good about
the *Gospel of Thomas* are those quotes that come directly
from the New Testament, and what is obscure and silli-
ness are those that do not.

The Gospel of Mary
Though not a specific part of the Nag Hammadi writings, we will look at *The Gospel of Mary* because of its
significance in *The Da Vinci Code*. It is also a part of Elaine

95

Pagels' *The Gnostic Gospels*, and references are made to this book by Mr. Brown. *The Gospel of Mary* was originally written in Greek. The two copies that are extant are extremely fragmentary. The early copy compromises only a "fragmentary leaf written in Greek dated in the early third century."[38] The longer, more complete version is a Coptic codex, the Berolinensis 8502, but considerable portions of that text are missing, as well. *The Gospel of Mary* is popular among feminist theologians, because in it, Mary Magdalene is portrayed as the Savior's beloved who possesses knowledge and teachings superior to that of the "public apostolic tradition."[39]

What we have of *The Gospel of Mary* is a very short dialogue between Mary and the apostles Peter, Levi and Andrew. In the beginning of the dialogue, Christ is quoted as saying, "All natures, all formations, all creatures exist in and with one another and they will be resolved again into their own roots."[40] The book of Revelation is quoted in it with Jesus saying, "He who has ears to hear let him hear."[41] In this dialogue, Mary then stands before Peter and Andrew and tells them of a rather ambiguous and obscure vision she had concerning Christ. After detailing her vision, Peter is somewhat distressed because Jesus apparently elects to visit a woman with a vision and not a man. Levi attempts to assuage some of Peter's consternation, pointing out that, "Surely the Savior knows her very well. That is why he loved her more than us."[42] This is the part that the "neo-Gnostics" and feminist theologians especially like about *The Gospel of Mary*.

Again, just as pointed out in the other two Gnostic "gospels," *The Gospel of Mary* was not written contemporaneously with the New Testament, as New Testament passages are quoted within this short text. Furthermore, it is again an example of pseudepigraphy and contains Gnostic jargon and theology when alluding to the pantheistic idea that all nature "exists in and with one another." In it Jesus states, "There is no sin, but it is in you who makes sin when you do the things that are like the nature of adultery, which is called sin."[43] It should be noted, nowhere in the text of this writing is the concept of Christ and Mary Magdalene being husband and wife mentioned. In fact, the Mary in this scripture is assumed to be Mary Magdalene, but is not described so in the text.

These then are three specific examples of Gnostic writings, two of which come from the Nag Hammadi, and one that comes from alternate sources. They are certainly examples of Gnostic Christian writings that incorporate Christ into the Gnostic myth. It is not our purpose to review all the Gnostic scriptures, but these have been selected due to their importance in *The Da Vinci Code*. Once again, I think it would be good for the reader to read the Gnostic writings for themselves and compare them with New Testament Scripture. Some of the Gnostic writings tell the Gnostic myth, some contain Gnostic poetry, and some, especially the "Gospel of Truth," probably written by the second-century Gnostic Valentinus, incorporate Gnostic jargon and Gnostic beliefs into Christian precepts. Some are Gnostic proverbs, and some are supposed sayings of Christ, but none of the Gnostics writings give a narrative description of Christ's life, and they are not "gospels" as we know them. They were all written after the New Testament writers had given us the gospels, the book of Acts, and the epistles, and none were written contemporaneously with the original New Testament.

The Gnostic Gospels

Before leaving the subject of Gnosticism, I would like to take a brief look at Elaine Pagels' *The Gnostic Gospels*. In Ms. Pagels' book, we are given a rose-tinted view of Gnosticism. Ms. Pagels does not go into great detail regarding Gnostic theology or Gnostic cosmology, the reason for which I am not fully sure. One reason might be because the readers could understand from more detail why Gnosticism was universally rejected by orthodox Christians in the first and second century. Instead, she gives us a glossed-over version of Gnosticism and prefers to refer more to those texts that deal with Mary Magdalene and passages that seem to promote a liberal feminist agenda. For example, in her introduction, she admits that Gnostic Christians "expressed ideas that the orthodoxed abhorred" but points out that "Christianity as the Apostolic creed defines, it contains some ideas that many of us today might find even stranger."[44] By this she is referring to the virgin birth of Jesus Christ, the deity of Christ, and His resurrection. Obviously Ms. Pagels denies these concepts. Instead, she believes the deity of Christ with His virgin birth and resurrection are allegorical in nature. This is part of the "greatest story ever sold" alluded to in *The Da Vinci Code*. In fact, Ms. Pagels refers to the New Testament gospels as "theory" and points out that Gnostics held the literal view of the resurrection as "faith of fools."[45]

Ms. Pagels makes a good point in her book, stating that like Baptist, Quakers, and many others, the Gnostics were convinced that whoever receives "spirit communications" communicates directly with the divine.[46] She also states that the apostles felt they alone held definitive religious authority and the canon of the New Testament was mostly determined by that apostolic authority.[47]

Ms. Pagels, I believe, makes a significant error, though, in equating first- and second-century early Christian writers, sometimes referred to as the early "fathers of Christianity," with having apostolic inspiration. I believe the New Testament certainly teaches against such an idea.

Apparently, Ms. Pagels also questions whether the crucifixion of Christ was an actual historical or literal event.[48] In fact, it is interesting to look at Ms. Pagels' view of the passion of Christ and the persecution of first-century Christians. After reading her discourse, Ms. Pagels would have us believing Christians actually desired their own martyrdom, and even apparently enjoyed it![49] Instead Ms. Pagels points out that the Gnostics viewed the crucifixion as "an occasion for discovering the divine self within" as she points out from *The Gospel of Truth*. Ms. Pagels states in her book, "I suggest that the persecution gave impetus to the formation of the organized church structure that developed by the end of the second century."[50] While persecution may have indeed given impetus to the success of the early church, it did so in spite of it and not because the first-century Christians desired it.

It is obvious that Ms. Pagels considers Gnosticism superior to New Testament theology. She refers to baptism and the partaking of the Lord's Supper as "the simplest essentials of faith" that would appeal to the masses, whereas the Gnostics' "higher level of Buddhist teaching" would appeal only to a few.[51]

It is clear then from Ms. Pagels' book, that although she claims to be "powerfully attracted to Christianity," she nonetheless places Gnostic Christianity on a par with traditional Christianity, with the Gnostic writings being at least as inspired and cogent as the New Testament.[52] Clearly Dan Brown incorporated a lot of Ms. Pagels' ideas in his book and in his character, Leigh Teabing. Sir Teabing even quotes Ms. Pagels when he says, "It is the winners who write history...!"[53]

Did the Gnostics Practice Heiros Gammos?

If you are like me, and you have read *The Da Vinci Code*, then the first time you encountered the words *heiros gammos* were in that novel. In *The Da Vinci Code*, Sophie, as a young woman, inadvertently walks in on her grandfather, Jacques Sauniere, while he is engaged in an act that is referred to as *heiros gammos*. The scene Mr. Brown depicts during this time is reminiscent of a scene from the movie *Eyes Wide Shut* by the late Stanley Kubrick. In *The Da Vinci Code*, Mr. Sauniere is engaged in sexual intercourse with a group of people surrounding him. Sophie, clearly at the time, has no clue what she is observing and it obviously traumatizes her, although there is no evidence from the book that she really discussed it with her grandfather. It is later explained to Sophie what she had witnessed was a religious act and part of a ceremonial ritual known as *heiros gammos*.

What is *heiros gammos*, and where did Dan Brown learn of it? According to Margaret Starbird and Lynn Picknett, *heiros gammos* is a premarital sexual act as mentioned earlier in this work. This was what was occurring with the anointing of the feet of Jesus as mentioned in the Gospels, according to Starbird and Picknett. Actually, *heiros gammos* is nothing more than temple prostitution prevalent in the Greek society of Jesus' day.

We see this in Acts 19. The Ephesians worshiped the pagan goddess Artemis, also known as Diana. Paul was causing a great disturbance in this town by evangelizing in the city of Ephesus and persuading many to turn away from this idolatrous religion. Involved in the worship of Diana were the temple prostitutes. Male worshipers had intercourse with the temple prostitutes, and this is essentially what is referred to as *heiros gammos*. From this worship of Diana also comes the concept of the "divine feminine." The "divine feminine" is nothing more than pagan worship and idolatry. With the act of *heiros gammos*, one was apparently reaching a state of ecstasy that put one closer to the goddess.

Some have equated this with the concept of "acquaintance" that occurs in Gnosticism.[54] Lynn Picknett and Clive Prince state in the *Templar Revelation* that it is through *heiros gammos* that the Gnostics could achieve "acquaintance."

After searching all the Gnostic scriptures, including those found in the Nag Hammadi, I find nothing that mentions the Gnostics practicing *heiros gammos*. Epiphanius of Salamis did mention the licentious behavior of the Gnostics in his treatise *Against Heresies*. Epiphanius, writing in the fourth century, described a sect of Gnostics known as the Borborites as consummating their passions through sexual intercourse.[55] Epiphanius is quoting from the Borborites writings when he states, "We are collecting the power of the vulgar from bodies by means of their emissions, that is by semen and menses."[56]

In that same work, Epiphanius stated that the Gnostic sect of the Borborites "hold their women in common." He also wrote about their "frenzied passion" and their "love feast."[58] He also alluded to homosexual acts that occurred within this Gnostic sect and even referred to acts of cannibalism and abortion performed by these Gnostics. The reliability of Epiphanius has been questioned by some authorities. This is because Epiphanius may have had a biased opinion of the Gnostics. Certainly it is very doubtful that all Gnostic sects engaged in these acts. Because this is the only source that mentions these activities, it appears this is where Ms. Starbird and Ms. Picknett associate *heiros gammos* with the Gnostics.

7
Can We Trust the Bible?

It has been stated by some that the reason for the immense popularity of *The Da Vinci Code* comes from the fact that we all love a good conspiracy story. That cannot be denied when one looks at American's propensity for believing conspiracies. For example, the assassination of John F. Kennedy has spawned many various conspiracy theories and resulted in numerous books, TV shows, and even full-length movies dealing with the subject. It is my belief, however, that the popularity of *The Da Vinci Code* goes far beyond simply its being a good conspiracy tale. I believe it would be very hard to attribute its success to that fact alone.

We live in a New Age society. New Age thought permeates the arts, music, literature, and religion. We live in a time where mysticism is embraced by many. The Bible is no longer considered the standard for authority. In fact, on the contrary, in this new age of ours, the Bible is now passé. Other books, other "scriptures," are considered at least as important, if not more important, than the Bible and considered equally inspired. Persons who believe that the Bible is the inspired Word of God are looked down upon as ignorant, uneducated, and out of touch with the changing society. We even have some so-called Christians now professing that for Christianity to survive in this new world, it must change and embrace this New Age liberal thinking.[1]

Exactly when this change occurred is hard to precisely state. People of my generation certainly remember the Beatles in their heyday going to India, meeting with the Maharishi, and bringing back to England a very mystic Hindu philosophy. Many of their songs were influenced by such mysticism. Remember the *Magical Mystery Tour*? A few years ago Shirley McClain wrote a book alluding to reincarnation. Her books have influenced many people. Other Hollywood actors, such as Richard Gere and Stephen Seagal, have embraced Buddhism, and its popularity has grown significantly. Sin, or the concept of right and wrong, has become relative. The ends justify the means. The current Broadway musical *Wicked*, although full of beautiful music, nonetheless has as its theme the relativity of evil.

Our society has taken on a very liberal point of view as it pertains to Jesus Christ and the Bible. We now have liberal judges determining that homosexual marriages, euphemistically referred to as "same-sex marriages," are legal in states such as Massachusetts and California. Abortion now is legal, and there are some who would like to even expand its definition. We have organizations such as PETA (People for the Ethical Treatment of Animals) who commit heinous crimes to promote the idea of equal rights for animals. Drug laws are being liberalized in many areas, and there are many who would like to see the use of illicit drugs made legal in this country. Freedom of speech is used by such organizations as the American Civil Liberties Union to justify pornography and obscenity over the public airways and in our literature. There is no longer any stigma attributed to men and women living together in a sexual relationship before marriage. In fact, sex education is being advocated to our youth in middle schools and high schools. Euthanasia is being promoted, and we have seen several current examples of human beings having their feeding tubes removed and essentially being starved to death because their lives have no more "dignity." All of these are examples of a deterioration in our society that I believe has come about from this New Age liberal movement.

Where there is no standard, the question then becomes, who determines what is right and what is wrong? If the Bible is no longer the book we use to determine these issues, and no other scriptures are used, then what *is* the method for how a judge determines that homosexual marriage is constitutional and, therefore, legal? The answer is that man himself becomes the sole determiner of right and wrong, moral and immoral, good and bad. This is a humanistic point of view. The Gnostics say it is through "acquaintance" and gaining insight that man is able to answer these questions, but they give no standard for which that insight is obtained. Certainly, the concept of sin is no longer appropriate in this new age of ours.[2] In fact, Gnosticism and New Age thought say that within each one of us is a divine spirit and that we are "all gods." As a result, we are surrounded by chaos today with a society that is spiraling down morally, ethically, and spiritually.

Dan Brown and his *Da Vinci Code* appear at this time and cast doubt on the tenets of Christianity. His book, along with many others, cast doubt on the divinity of Christ. They would have us believe that first-century Christians considered Jesus to be just a man and not the Son of God. We have pointed out that this is blatantly untrue. Further, they would have us believe that first-century Christians had multiple gospels from which to choose, and only the "winners" won. As a result, the Bible, as we have it today, was written by these winners. Again, it is hoped that this book has clearly shown this is not the case. What *The Da Vinci Code* has done, especially for those who are unstudied in the gospels and in the history of the Church, is to cast doubt and in some ways justify the use of man's reason as a standard for determining right and wrong. This, to me, explains a lot of the popularity of this book.

Conservative Christians should not be apologetic for the New Testament, and certainly there is nothing in *The Da Vinci Code* that should cause one's faith to waver. Mr. Brown's book is not the first book to attack the Bible, nor do I think it will be the last. The Bible is the most unique book in the history of mankind, and the evidence is overwhelming to support its inspiration from God. First, it was written over a span of some fifteen hundred years by more than forty authors coming from various walks of life including kings, military leaders, peasants, philosophers, fishermen, tax collectors, poets, musicians, statesmen, scholars, and shepherds. It was written in different places over different times and on three different continents. It was written in three languages, Hebrew, Aramaic, and Greek. The style of writing in the Bible includes poetry, historical narrative, psalms, personal correspondence, biography, prophecy, parable, and allegory. Hundreds of topics are treated by the Bible including marriage, divorce, homosexuality, adultery, obedience to authority, cheating, lying, stealing, parenting, and the nature and revelation of God.

Yet in spite of its immense diversity, the Bible presents a single unified story, that is, God's redemption of humankind. As Norman Geesler and William Nicks put it, the Paradise Lost of Genesis becomes the Paradise Regained of Revelation.[3] The one unifying theme throughout the book is man's salvation from sin through an unwavering faith and obedience to His Word, with the one leading character throughout the book, God, being known through His Son, Jesus Christ.

The number of Bibles in print over the years has reached well into the billions and each year alone there are over 21 million Bibles and some 20 million New Testaments distributed throughout the world. Ironically the only book to outsell *The Da Vinci Code* in the last two years has been the Bible![4] The Bible has been translated in over 2,200 languages, which represents the primary vehicle of communication for well over "90 percent of the world's population."[5] The Bible has weathered the test of time. There is more evidence to support the Bible than any "ten pieces of classical literature combined."[6] The emperor Diocletian, in 303 AD, issued an edict to stop Christianity and ordered all Bibles to be destroyed. Christianity progressed in spite of this, and ironically, as we have noted, in the year 325, Constantine, one of Diocletian's successors, would issue an edict to have some fifty copies of the New Testament created at the government's expense.

The Bible is unique in its prophetic works. Although the Koran, the Book of Mormon, and the Hindu Vedas are considered by their followers to be inspired, they contain no predictive prophecies. By contrast, the Old Testament contains hundreds of prophetic predictions that have come true and can be substantiated.

Mr. Lewis S. Chafer has said, "The Bible is not such a book a man would write if he could or could write if he would."[7] By that he means that the winners did not write the Bible. This is clearly seen in how the Bible frankly speaks of the sins of its characters. Look at the sins of the patriarchs, such as Abraham, Isaac, and Jacob. Look at the sins of King David and his adultery and subsequent murder due to his relationship with Bathsheba. The gospels point out the faults of the apostles, including the sins of Peter. Finally, the epistles point to the disorder that was within the church.[8] As can be seen, the Bible presents reality and not fantasy, the good parts with the bad.

We also have ample evidence of the historical accurateness and reliability of the New Testament. There are some 5,686 extant Greek manuscripts of the New Testament. There are some 19,284 extant manuscripts in the Latin Vulgate, Ethiopian, Slavic, Armenian, Syriac, and other languages. There are no other documents in antiquity that even approach these numbers. By comparison, Homer's *Iliad* contains only 643 manuscripts that are extant. And although no original copies of the New Testament exist today, that is, the original letters written by Paul or the original gospels, we do have a great number of manuscripts that are very close in time to the originals. There are some partial manuscripts of the New Testament that date back to the second century, meaning less than a hundred years after the original works were penned. By contrast, the earliest known manuscripts of most of the Greek classical authors date to a thousand years or more after their author's death. Compared to the over 5,000 Greek manuscripts of the New Testament, there is a distinct "poverty of manuscripts of some of the ancient documents."[9] As another example, Plato's works were written in about 400 BC, yet the earliest copies that we have of such works were written in 900 AD. That is a 1,300-year gap, and we only have seven copies of those documents. Still, Plato's works are read throughout the world, and no one doubts their authenticity.

As pointed out, the New Testament was in circulation long before the Council of Nicea met in 325 AD, contrary to what is reported in Mr. Brown's book. The evidence for this early circulation date is found in the overwhelming support to their existence by the quotations of the early Christian writers such as Justin Martyr, Irenaeus, Clement, Origen, Tertullian, Hippolytus, and Eusebius. Their writings quote some 36,289 passages from the New Testament, including from the gospels, the book of Acts, Paul's epistles, the other general epistles, and the book of Revelation. These men all lived well before Constantine, and it should be pointed out that there are over 32,000 citations of the New Testament prior to the time of the Counsel of Nicea in 325 AD. Finally, Ignatius, who lived between 70 and 110 AD, was an elder at the church in Antioch, knew the apostles personally, and quoted from Matthew, John, Acts, Romans, 1 Corinthians, Galatians, Ephesians, Philippians, Colossians, 1 and 2 Thessalonians, 1 and 2 Timothy, James, and 1 Peter in his seven books.[10] These internal evidences alone certainly do not prove the inspiration of the New Testament, but they do give credence to its reliability and its authenticity.

There are also some who doubt the historical accurateness of the existence of Jesus Christ, the man. External evidence overwhelmingly supports the historicity of Jesus Christ. A first-century Roman by the name of Tacitus spoke of the persecution of Christ. Suetonius, a chief secretary to Emperor Hadrian, reported about the disturbance in Jerusalem regarding Christ and His followers.[11] Josephus writings in 77 to 78 AD spoke of Jesus and referred to Him as the Christ and as one who had drawn to Him "both many of the Jews and many of the Gentiles." He even spoke of Christ's crucifixion and His "alleged" resurrection on the third day.[12] Other examples could be cited, but suffice it to say that the historicity is confirmed by both Christians and pagans (that is non-Christians and non-Jews), even those who would usually be considered antagonistic toward Christianity. We should have no doubt that Jesus Christ lived and breathed on this earth.

Finally, Christianity lives or dies based on the resurrection of Jesus Christ. If Christ did not rise from the dead, then Paul accurately states "that we are of all men most pitiable."[13] Admittedly, the belief in the resurrection of Jesus Christ is the foundation for the faith of all Christians. If the resurrection were a hoax or a delusion or a figment of the disciples' imagination, then Christianity is vain, and Christ is not the Son of God, who He claimed to be. No other prominent founders of religions such as Buddha, Mohammed, or Confucius can claim a bodily resurrection. In this regard, Christ is unique. Christ, therefore, both predicted His death and His resurrection.[14] If one has faith in the reliability of the New Testament, one cannot doubt the resurrection of Jesus Christ.

But is there historical evidence of the resurrection of Jesus Christ? Luke, who was an eyewitness to the life of Jesus Christ, stated that Jesus showed Himself alive by many "infallible proofs," an expression indicating the "strongest type of legal evidence."[15] Luke stated in the preface to his gospel that he gathered his information from eyewitnesses to the life of Jesus Christ. Using the pronoun *we*, Luke was himself a participator in some of the events that he narrated. Luke gave unique and precise details of the resurrection of Jesus Christ, telling us that it was witnessed by His disciples and literally hundreds of others. Quoting Faust Wescott, an English scholar in the late nineteenth century who was appointed Regius professor at Cambridge in 1870, "in deed, taking all the evidence together, it is not too much to say that there is no historic incident better or more variously supported than the resurrection of Christ. Nothing but the antecedent assumption that it must be false could have suggested the idea of deficiency in the proof of it."[16] Further, the resurrection of Christ was never doubted by first-century Christians as supported by writings of early church leaders. The historical facts are that Jesus died a cruel death on the cross and was buried in a cave or a rock-hewn tomb. That tomb was sealed with a very large stone called a *golel*. It then was guarded by a group of Roman guards with the penalty of death if they fell asleep or forsook their responsibilities.

In spite of this, on the third day after Christ's burial, the guards found an empty tomb, which was an undisputable fact. The chief priest and elders bribed the solders guarding the tomb and instructed them to say that they had fallen asleep as the explanation to the missing body. After His resurrection, Christ appeared first to Mary Magdalene and to the other women returning to the tomb, and later to Peter and to the Emmaus disciples, as well as Thomas. He then appeared to over 500-plus believers on the Galilean mountain, as reported by Paul in 1 Corinthians. His ascension was witnessed by his disciples in Acts 1, and later Christ appeared to Paul and Stephen. He finally appeared to John on the island of Patmos, as described in the book of Revelation.

Many have made light of the resurrection of Jesus Christ, and as Elaine Pagels has stated, "think it strange." They have offered various explanations, all of which fail miserably in disproving the resurrection of Christ. Some have proposed a "swoon theory," stating that when Christ was placed in the tomb of Joseph of Arimathea, He was actually still alive. Certainly His disciples did not see Him as merely swooning, and the description of the wound in His side would reveal that His blood had already congealed with His serum, indicating that He had died.

Others have postulated the "theft theory," stating that Jesus' body was stolen from the tomb. This is, in fact, what Matthew alluded to in his gospel when he stated that the elders had tried to convince the guards to tell the people that when they were asleep, His disciples came in at night and stole Him away.[17] For this, the guards were bribed by the Jewish elders. Obviously, the Roman soldiers did not know how to explain the empty tomb and were told by the Sanhedrin leaders to concoct this story.

The theft theory does not hold up, either. First, His disciples would not be empowered to steal the body of Christ. Most of them had fled during His crucifixion, and they did not really understand the prophecy regarding His resurrection. Furthermore, they would not have been able to overcome the Roman soldiers to take His body. Also, the grave clothes at the site of His burial give testimony to His resurrection. As Merle Teeny remarks, "No robbers would have rewound the wrappings in their original shape, for there would have been no time to do so, they would have flung the clothes down in disorder and fled with the body."[18] It is especially hard to believe that His disciples would have stolen His body and then, with the exception of John, die a martyr's death for this great lie that they were perpetuating. As Paul Little writes, "Men will die for what they believe to be true though they may actually be false: they do not however die for what they know is a lie."[19] John R. W. Scott also states, "Hypocrites and martyrs are not made of the same stuff."[20] So, when one looks at the empty tomb, there are really only two feasible explanations. One is that the body was removed by human hands, therefore, either removed by the enemies of Christ, for which there was no motive, or removed by His friends or disciples, for which they had no power, or the empty tomb was the result of a divine work, which is the most logical of explanations.

There is also the "hallucination theory," which is a very popular theory today and apparently the one believed by Ms. Pagels.[21] In this theory, all post-resurrection appearances by Christ were actually no more than examples of hallucinations, and mass hallucinations at that. In other words, His disciples desired His resurrection so badly that they had hallucinations concerning His resurrection and actually believed these hallucinations to be true. This is an incredible doctrine and does not follow any known psychiatric or psychological theory or experiences. You simply do not see five hundred people having the same hallucination at the same time with the same experiences. There are some evidences in the past of assemblies having visions, but in these cases, they are always accompanied by a "morbid excitement of the mental life, as well as by a morbid bodily condition, especially by nervous affection."[22] Again, Luke, a physician, a man who would be accustomed to scientifically considering a given subject, wrote in the book of Acts that the Lord "showed himself alive after his passing by many infallible proofs." Human eyes saw the bodily resurrection of Jesus Christ, human hands touched the body of Christ, and human ears heard the voice of Christ. These were not mere hallucinations. Jesus also ate a piece of boiled fish ostensibly to show His bodily resurrection.[23] Also, the disciples not only saw Christ but conversed with Him at various times and circumstances and with various witnesses, which is contrary to how hallucinations occur. Christ's disciples had not even expected His resurrection and, in fact, had gone back to their jobs of fishing and were somewhat surprised when His resurrection did occur. This simply does not jive with the hallucination theory.

Finally, there is the idea that the women, and subsequently the rest of the disciples, simply went to the wrong tomb after Jesus was buried. This is very unlikely as Mary Magdalene and the other Mary had witnessed the burial of Christ. It would have been very unlikely that they would have gone back to the wrong tomb. Furthermore, there was an angel sitting at the tomb when they came back to confirm that it was the burial site of Jesus. Also, if the women went to the wrong tomb, then why would the Sanhedrin be so upset about the risen body of Jesus Christ? It is simply preposterous to think that Mary and the other disciples went to the wrong tomb.

In summary, Jesus prophesied that He would be persecuted, crucified, and then raised on the third day. The Pharisees understood this and warned Pilate.[24] For that reason, Pilate put Roman guards around the tomb of Christ and had it secured with a great stone and seal. Roman guards then guarded the tomb of Jesus Christ to prevent His disciples from coming in to steal the body. As the New Testament confirms, an angel of the Lord descended and rolled the stone away, and the risen body of Jesus walked away from the tomb.[25]

The first witnesses of Jesus Christ's resurrection were Mary Magdalene, Mary the mother of James, and Salome.[26] Jesus then appeared to His apostles later that day. In the book of Acts, Luke stated that Christ remained on the earth and appeared to His disciples for a period of forty days. Jesus proved His resurrection to even those who doubted. The gospel of John tells us that Thomas did not initially believe the disciples when they told him of Christ's resurrection. Thomas eventually saw the risen Savior with his own eyes and proclaimed Him Lord and God.[27] Again, the apostles and writers of the New Testament were eyewitnesses to Jesus' ministry on earth. The miracles He performed, and finally His resurrection and ascension, proved His deity. It cannot be denied that to believe this now requires a significant amount of faith. But just as Jesus told Thomas, "Because you have seen me you have believed? Blessed are they who did not see and yet believed," so Christians today who have the faith that Jesus is the Son of God can feel comfort in being blessed.[28]

The conclusion can only be that Christ, indeed, is risen. Certainly, first-century Christians believed this. In his letter to the Romans, Paul stated that Christ "was declared to be the Son of God with power according to the Spirit of Holiness, by the resurrection from the dead."[29]

8
The Problem With Diversity

In *The Da Vinci Code*, Dan Brown writes that early Christians were a very diverse group. He points out in Chapter 55 of his book that the Emperor Constantine attempted to consolidate the Roman government under one religion, Christianity. Elaine Pagels, in her book, *The Gnostic Gospels*, also addressed this idea of diversity. She states that "early Christianity is far more diverse than nearly anyone expected from the Nag Hammadi discoveries."[1] Those Nag Hammadi discoveries are, of course, the Gnostic Gospels that were discussed in a previous chapter. Interestingly, Dan Brown would include early Christian writings in the Dead Sea Scrolls.[2] Clearly the Dead Sea Scrolls were not Christian at all, and the Dead Sea Scrolls and the Nag Hammadi writings were not the earliest Christian records, as Mr. Brown states through his character Teabing in *The Da Vinci Code*.[3]

One cannot deny that contemporary Christianity is a very diverse and complex religion, and it would not be surprising that early Christianity was also diverse. It is equally clear that diversity is not what the New Testament writers intended. There is a point to be made when one looks to the diversity of Christianity and tries to justify the diversity historically. That point,however, has no validity. Paul stated in his first letter to the Corinthians, "Now I exhort you brethren by the name of our Lord Jesus Christ that you all agree, and there be no divisions among you but you be made complete in the same mind in the same judgement."[4] In his letter to Christians, Jude warned that certain persons had "crept in un-noticed, those who were long before hand marked out for this condemnation, ungodly persons who turn the grace of our God into licentiousness and deny our only Master and Lord Jesus Christ."[5] The apostle Peter in his second letter told the brethren that just as there were false prophets before, there would also be "false teachers among you who will secretly introduce destructive heresies even denying the Master who bought them bringing swift destruction upon themselves."[6]

As one can see, there were already the beginnings of division occurring in the first-century church. But again, it was never the intent for Christianity to be so diverse. Jesus prayed in John 17 that His disciples would be "sanctified in truth," and also that "they all may be one even as Thou Father art in Me and I in Thee. That they also be in us and that the world may believe that Thou did send me."[7] Paul in his letter to the Galatians warned the brethren not to desert from the gospel that was taught to them for a "different Gospel."[8] He also warned in the same chapter, "even though we are an angel from heaven should preach to you a Gospel contrary to that which we have preached to you let him be a cursed. As we have said before so I say again, if any man is preaching to you a Gospel contrary to that which you receive let him be accursed."[9] As these scriptures show, it would not be surprising to find various sects of Christianity emerging in the first and second centuries. Such sects would include the Gnostics, whose theology actually predated Christianity but who tried to incorporate Christianity into their religion; the Ebionites, who have been called Christians "still climbing out of a Jewish shell;" and the Marcionites, who sought to completely rid themselves of the Jewish heritage even to the point of looking to the Jewish God as a God that had failed. By the time Constantine called together the Council of Nicea in 325 AD, the biggest ongoing controversy concerned the Arians, followers of Arius who disputed the notion that Jesus was of the same substance as the Father.

One might ask, with all this diversity, how could one decide who in fact had the truth versus those "deceivers" mentioned in Ephesians 5?[10] The answer in a word is, *miracles*!

Neither Christ nor His apostles expected their followers to accept what they said on blind faith alone. The words that the apostles taught were confirmed by miraculous signs.[11] Paul wrote to the Thessalonians, "Our gospel did not come to you in word only, but also in power and in the Holy Spirit and with full conviction...."[12] The very purpose of the miracles performed by Jesus were to confirm that He was the Son of God. John 20:30 states, "Many other signs therefore Jesus also performed in the presence of the Disciples, which are not written in this Book but they have been written that you may believe that Jesus

is the Christ, the Son of God and that believing you may
have life in His name." The faith of Christianity, then, is
largely a faith that is based upon the miraculous works
performed by both Jesus and His disciples.

One might ask, where are miracles today to confirm
that the Bible is still the Word of God? Again, the purpose of miracles was to confirm the Word by those
teaching the gospel in the first century. Because there was
no New Testament to circulate among the brethren, the
way a first-century Christian could discern what was truth
versus what was a deception was through miracles. When
the canon of the New Testament finally came together,
the purpose of the miracles would cease. I believe that in
1 Corinthians 13, Paul was referring to this. Paul wrote,
"For we know in part and we prophesy in part but when
the perfect comes the partial will be done away."[13] There
would be no need for miraculous works once the New
Testament was put into writing. One can see that these
miracles would cease after the first century because only
the apostles received the gift of miracles firsthand. Others who received the miraculous gifts of the Holy Spirit
received them only through the laying on of hands by the
apostles. Simon the Sorcerer recognized this in Acts 8
when he "saw that the spirit was bestowed through the
laying on of the apostles' hands...."[14] The Christians in
Corinth did not receive the miraculous gifts of the Holy
Spirit until after they were baptized and Paul had "laid
his hands upon them."[15] It should be noted that only the
apostles received the miraculous gifts of the Holy Spirit
directly, with the exception of Cornelius in Acts 10, who
received the gift of the Holy Spirit directly in order to
show that the Gentiles were equally entitled to the saving grace of Jesus Christ.[16] It should also be pointed out

that these miraculous gifts could only be transferred to
someone else through the laying on of hands by the
apostles and those who received such gifts could not im-
part them to someone else.[17]

By the time those Christians who had received miraculous gifts through the laying on of hands of the
apostles had died, the gospels and much of the epistles
would have been in circulation. As we have pointed out
earlier, the core of the New Testament, that is, the four
gospels and the thirteen letters of Paul, were accepted
and in circulation as early as 130 AD.[18] At that time, Christians would have a document to compare with
teachings that might be brought in by false teachers
and deceivers. They could compare and decide
whether the new teachings coincided with the Scriptures they possessed. Paul told the Corinthians that
it was "not surprising if his servants (Satan's) also
disguise themselves as servants of righteousness
whose end shall be according to their deeds."[19] He
described such men as false apostles, deceitful work-
ers disguising themselves as apostles of Christ.[20]

Of course, the ultimate miracle to confirm that Jesus
was the Son of God occurred in His resurrection. Paul
told the Corinthians in his first letter, "That if there is no
resurrection of the dead, not even Christ has been raised:
and if Christ has not been raised then our preaching is in
vain and our faith is also in vain."[21] As stated previously,
without the resurrection of Jesus Christ, Christianity is a
fraud, and as Paul stated, vain, and our faith then becomes
"worthless." Finally, in the same chapter, Paul wrote, "If
we have hope in Christ in this life only, we are all men
most to be pitied."[22]

The belief that Jesus Christ was raised on the third day of course requires faith on our part, but we are not left without significant evidence that it occurred. As we pointed out in the previous chapter, the writers of the New Testament were eyewitnesses to Jesus, to His miracles, and to His resurrection. Peter in his second epistle stated, "For we did not follow cleverly devised tales when we made known to you the power in coming of our Lord Jesus Christ, but we were eyewitnesses of His majesty."[23] At the Transfiguration of Jesus Christ, a voice from heaven came and said, "This is My beloved Son in whom I am well pleased: Listen to him!"[24] Peter, along with James and John, were eyewitnesses to this event and heard the voice that made this majestic statement; Peter wrote again in his second epistle, "That we ourselves heard this utterance made from heaven when we were with Him in the holy mountain."[25]

Although Dan Brown's character Teabing is right in stating that the Bible did not come down from a fax from heaven,[26] it is an absurd notion that the Bible is a product of the "winners" in that the "winners" determined the canon of the New Testament.[27] I believe that Paul is correct when he stated in 2 Timothy that "all scripture is inspired by God and profitable for teaching, for reproof, for correction, for training and righteousness; that the man of God maybe be equipped for every good work."[28]

The fact that Christianity survived at all is proof of the Providence of God and the inspiration of the New Testament. Dan Brown wants us to believe it was because of the Roman government that Christianity grew. In fact, the Roman government did everything it could to destroy Christianity, which is a matter of historical record. Christians from the first century on were severely persecuted, tortured, imprisoned, and murdered for the cause of Christ. It makes no sense at all that the writers of the New Testament were perpetuating a myth or a lie and that they would be willing to die for this. As stated in the previous chapter, if the New Testament was written by the "winners," then why are there human flaws brought out by its writers? Paul called himself "foremost of all sinners."[29] The denial of Peter at Jesus' crucifixion is well-documented in the gospels. Further, Paul chastised Peter to his face for his hypocrisy.[30] So, it makes no sense, and it is a preposterous notion for anyone to believe that the New Testament was written three centuries after the death of Christ by the so-called winners. Not only does history tell us that most, if not all, of the apostles were crucified for their belief in Jesus Christ, but thousands upon thousands more died for their belief in the deity of Christ at the hands of the Roman government. In spite of this, Christianity *did* survive until the time of Constantine, and the conversion of Constantine to Christianity no doubt played a significant part in the spread of Christianity at that time.

A Question of Faith

In the end it really becomes a question of faith. It becomes a question of whether or not one believes that Jesus Christ actually walked on the face of the earth. It becomes a question of whether or not Jesus was who He claimed to be, the Son of God. It becomes a question of whether or not one believes that He did the miracles to prove His divinity. It becomes a question of whether or not one believes that He died on the cross and was resurrected three days later. It becomes a question of whether or not one believes that the Holy Spirit was imparted to His apostles to convey the Word to the world, and therefore save a corrupt world from its sins. It becomes a question of whether or not one believes that the Holy Spirit inspired such men to write the words of God down and whether or not we have those words now in the form of the New Testament. It also then becomes a question of whether or not one believes that the gospel is sufficient and that the gospel "was once for all delivered to the saints."[31]

Paul in his letter to the Romans wrote that it is through faith that we are justified.[32] That faith then comes by hearing and by hearing "the Word of God."[33] Because the New Testament writers are no longer around, that "hearing" would be in written form (i.e., the New Testament). Hebrews 11:1 defines faith as "the assurance of things hoped for, the conviction of things not seen." The writer of Hebrews also states that "without faith it is impossible to please him, for he who comes to God must believe that he exists and that he is the rewarder of those who seek him."[34] The book of Hebrews goes on to show the many examples of faith in the Old Testament that were manifested by obedience to God.

The book of Revelation was written primarily to first-century Christians who were about to undergo extreme persecution by the Roman government. It was written to show that eventually Christians and Christ would win the great battle against Satan. In Revelation 2:10, Christ told the brethren at Smyrna to "be faithful until death and I will give you a crown of life." This is the kind of faith that God demands of us, a faith that indeed will allow us to undergo persecutions and trials and remain steadfast to the end.

Christians, therefore, need not be ashamed of the gospel as Paul affirmed.[35] Christians need not be concerned about newfound "gospels" or concerned about latter-day revelations. We can be assured that we have the Word of God in the form of the New Testament.

There are those who would wish to confuse and distort the gospel, and there will always be such men and women, as the New Testament forewarns. We need to get back to the Bible, to study its teachings, and to do as Paul commanded Timothy, "Be diligent to present yourself approved to God as a workman who does not need to be ashamed handling accurately the word of truth."[36]

In doing this, one comes to the conclusion that Christianity should not be diverse but should be one. Paul told the Ephesians, "There is one body and one spirit just as also you were called in one hope of your calling, one Lord, one faith, one Baptism, one God and Father of all who is overall, through all and in all."[37] It was Christ's intention that Christians would all believe the same doctrine and obey the same principles laid out in the New Testament. There was never any intention for there to be divided Christians as we see today.

It is this problem in diversity that I believe causes some to doubt the validity of Christianity. When one sees the different beliefs, the different practices, the different types of baptism, and the different types of worship that are so varied within the Christian community, one may come to the belief that we cannot know the truth and, therefore, any faith is acceptable as long as one is "sincere about it." As the above scriptures have pointed out, this is not the desire of Christ. Jesus said, "You shall know the truth and the truth shall make you free."[38] In the book of Revelation, John, through the Holy Spirit, wrote, "If anyone takes away from the words of the Book of this Prophecy, God shall take away his part from the tree of life and from the Holy city, which is written in this Book."[39] Paul wrote to the Philippians, "Make my joy complete by being of the same mind, maintaining the same love, united in spirit and intent on one purpose."[40] Paul also stated that eventually, at the name of Jesus, "every knee should bow of those who are in earth and on earth and under earth and every tongue should confess that Jesus Christ is Lord to the glory of God the Father."[41] It is incumbent upon us all to come to that knowledge before this life is over, rather than to wait until it is too late.

Is *The Da Vinci Code* Dangerous?

We have seen that *The Da Vinci Code* is full of lies and great distortions. No, Jesus was not married to Mary Magdalene. And no, Mary was not the successor to Christ on earth, as there *was* no successor to Christ on earth. And no, first-century Christians did not have over eighty gospels to choose from. And no, the "winners" did not write the gospel. And no, the Gnostic gospels are not inspired scriptures, and they are not to be compared to the New Testament. And no, there is no secret society holding some ancient relic that would destroy Christianity.

There are many today who would attempt to place stumbling blocks in front of Christians and dissuade those of a conservative view that Jesus was the Son of God and that the Bible is the holy, inspired Word of God. At the beginning of this book, I called *The Da Vinci Code* "dangerous," and it is for this reason I did so. I fear Mr. Brown's book may cause some to lose their souls, and that indeed makes it supremely dangerous! Jesus warned of those who would do so when He stated, "It would be better for him if a millstone were hung around his neck and he were thrown into the sea than that he should cause one of these little ones to stumble."[42] As a result, Christ warned us to be on guard. I believe that it is now time for Christians to take a stand in what they believe. It is through the Providence of God that we have the Bible. The Bible is the standard by which man should make decisions concerning morality and what is right and wrong. I believe that we can read the Bible and come to a unity of faith.

Appendix I:
The Mystery of Rennes-Le-Château and Bérenger Saunière

Although not expressly mentioned in *The Da Vinci Code*, the mystery of Rennes-Le-Château permeates *The Da Vinci Code*. In fact, to a large extent, it is the basis for the book. The character Jacques Sauniére's name is inspired by the Bérenger Sauniére, the curé of the church at the village of Rennes-Le-Château. Because of its importance to *The Da Vinci Code*, a brief discussion of the mystery will be given. *Holy Blood, Holy Grail* begins with a discussion of the mystery of Rennes-Le-Château. Picknett and Prince also discuss the mystery extensively in the book *The Templar Revelation*. Readers can refer to those two books for a detailed discussion of the so-called mystery. What follows is a more thumbnail sketch.

The story goes like this. In 1885, a French village by the name of Rennes-Le-Château was sent a new priest by the name of Bérenger Sauniére. Rennes-Le-Château is in an area of France known as the Languedoc, close to the town of Limoux. Rennes-Le-Château was once a major Visigothic stronghold and eventually become an area where many of the Knights Templar took residence. At the age of 33, Bérenger Sauniére became priest of the church at Rennes-Le-Château. From the years 1885 to 1891, Sauniére's income was approximately six pounds sterling a year. During this time, he became very well-acquainted with a young girl by the name of Marie Denarnaud, at that time eighteen years old. She became his housekeeper and eventually a lifelong companion.

In 1891, Sauniére began a restoration of the village church. In removing the altar of the church during the restoration, Sauniére supposedly found four parchments with genealogies that dated from 1244 and 1644, with the other two dating from 1780. Contained in these parchments, as the mystery goes, were ciphers, or codes. As a result of this discovery, Sauniére was sent to Paris to present the parchments to Abbé Bieil, director general of the seminary of Saint Sulpice. Apparently Sauniére spent some three weeks in Paris and met many interesting individuals there, such as Émile Hoffet, the composer Claude de Bussy, the diva Emma Calvé, as well as many other characters. Sauniére also spent some time in the Louvre museum and apparently purchased three paintings at that time.

In any event, Sauniére eventually returned to the village of Rennes-Le-Château, and from there, the mystery really begins. For some unexplained reason, and hence the mystery, Sauniére began spending enormous amounts of money beginning in about 1896. By the end of his life in 1917, Sauniére had spent the equivalent of several million pounds in the restoration of the church at Rennes-Le-Château. He also spent money on his personal residence there, as well as spending money on public works and restoring the tower of the church, the "Tower Magdala."

While at the village, Sauniére received many notable visitors, including the Archduke, Johann Von Hapsburg, cousin of Franz Joseph, emperor of Austria. During his lifetime, Sauniére never explained his wealth. He confided his parchments to the seminary of Saint Sulpice. When he died in 1919, he died penniless, having transferred his wealth to Marie Denarnaud. When she died in 1953, she carried the secrets of Sauniére's wealth to her grave. The mystery, then, is, how did Sauniére accumulate such wealth and what happened to his wealth at his death or the death of Marie Denarnaud?

This is where speculation becomes rampant. In the book *Holy Blood, Holy Grail*, the authors present several theories. Could Sauniére have simply discovered vast treasure at the village church? Could Sauniére have discovered in these parchments codes that would allude to some sort of secret knowledge? Could this knowledge have been used to blackmail someone or some organization, such as the Catholic Church? Could Sauniére's wealth have been a payment for his silence?[1] Baigent, Leigh, and Lincoln even speculate that Sauniére could have been blackmailing the Vatican! Some have postulated that buried at the church was either treasure or relics that would damage the reputation and the fundamental precepts of the church. Some have even suggested that the remains of Mary Magdalene are buried at the church. Again, all of this is sheer speculation. I believe that the "sangreal documents" to which Mr. Brown alludes in *The Da Vinci Code* are derived from these notions. So much for the mystery, now for the truth.

Abbé Sauniére, whose wealth had probably been greatly overexaggerated, was suspended by his bishop in 1911 for "selling overbooked masses."[2] Furthermore, the parchments that were found by Sauniére proved to be fake, and the so-called mystery was in actuality an invention by a local restaurateur in the 1950s to attract tourists![3] Sauniére's wealth came from selling these overbooked masses. And needless to say, no relics, although they have been assiduously looked for, have ever been found at the church at Rennes-Le-Château!

Appendix II:
Similarities between Gnosticism, Hinduism, and Buddhism

In Gnosticism we have the first principle, and in Hinduism the only true reality is the Brahma. Just as in Gnosticism the first principle is self-existent, infinite, and omnipresent, so is the Brahma in Hinduism. Through meditation, one becomes united with the Brahma, much as through acquaintance one becomes united with the first principle. Hindus believe in "transmigration of the soul," in other words reincarnation, which is also a Gnostic concept. Hindus do not believe in a personal almighty god or creator, or ruler of all things. They furthermore lack a true conception of moral obligation, moral law, or sin. Salvation is from unreality rather than from sin, just as salvation in Gnosticism is through acquaintance or gnosis and not through a forgiveness of sin. In Hinduism, there is no savior who sacrificed himself for the salvation of man's sins, just at the Gnostics believed that Christ's crucifixion was for achieving acquaintance and not salvation from sin.

Buddhism, which had its origins in Hinduism, also shows distinct similarities to Gnosticism. The Gautama Buddha had his epiphany under the Bo tree, or "knowledge tree." His way to spirituality was through "nirvana," which involves the loss of all individual consciousness and existence, an absorption into the "all." This is very similar to the Gnostics' ideal of "acquaintance." It is through right meditation or absorption that one assures entrance into nirvana at death, according to the Buddha. Again, as in Hinduism, there is no concept of sin, nor a concept of a need for forgiveness of sin, and certainly no concept of a need for a sacrifice for our sins in the Buddhist theology.

It also should be noted that the Gnostics were an elitist group, a "we-are-the-only-ones-going-to-heaven" group, if you will. In this fashion, they were Calvinist before the birth of John Calvin in that they believed only the descendants of Seth, who were a pre-elect or ordained group of people, would achieve *Gnosis* and, therefore, achieve "salvation." However, they were not completely Calvinistic because they also believed in a falling from grace. The apostate Gnostics were condemned and were not reincarnated, but were rather saved for a "greater punishment." In other words, a Gnostic could fall from grace!

Appendix III:
Assertions and Arguments

The Da Vinci Code Assertions

1. Mary Magdalene and Jesus were married.
2. Jesus appointed Mary as His successor.
3. Mary bore the child of Christ.
4. A male-dominated Church suppressed Mary and women.
5. Mary (along with Joseph of Arimethea) fled to Gaul (France).
6. Mary was the Holy Grail (sangreal), or bloodline, of Jesus.
7. The Merovengians (kings of France) were descendants of Jesus and Mary.
8. The Merovengian's [Mer-ven (Mary, the vine)] lineage persists to this day.

9. The Priory of Sion, formed in the Middle Ages with the Knights Templar, their militant arm, protects the "sangreal documents."
10. The Catholic Church seeks to keep the sangreal documents from the public.
11. The Priory is waiting for the "right time" to divulge the documents.

More *Da Vinci Code* Assertions

1. Church fathers sought to squelch a matriarchal pagan society and change it into a patriarchal Christian society.
2. These fathers ignored some eighty early gospels and rewrote the Bible.
3. The Council of Nicae under Constantine met to deify Christ and rewrite the Bible.
4. For centuries, the Church has persecuted women, and during the Inquisition, had over 5 million burned at the stake.

Mary Magdalene of *The Da Vinci Code*

1. Pagan priestess from Egypt
2. Lover of Jesus
3. Anointed Jesus in a pagan rite of *heiros gammos*
4. Became head of the Christian Church after Christ's death
5. Eventually fled to France
6. Gnostic "gospels" prove the relationship of Jesus and Mary
7. *The Gospel of Phillip* calls Mary Christ's companion and says that He kissed her often on the mouth.
8. *The Gospel of Mary* suggests that Jesus gave Mary special revelation. Peter was jealous of her.

Appendix III

The Mary Magdalene of the Bible
1. Was exorcised of seven demons by Christ (*Luke 8:2*)
2. Contributed financially to Jesus and His apostles (*Luke 20:1*)
3. Ministered to Jesus (*Matthew 27:53*)
4. Witnessed His crucifixion (*Matthew 22:55; John 19:25*)
5. Saw the burial of Christ (*Matthew 27:61*)
6. Came to anoint the body of Christ, saw an empty tomb (*Matthew 28:1; Mark 16:1; Luke 24:1–10; John 20:1*)
7. Was the first to see the resurrected Savior (*Mark 16:9*)
8. Worshiped the risen Savior (*Matthew 28:9*)
9. Reported Christ's resurrection to the apostles (*Mark 16:10; Luke 24:10; John 20:18*): "I have seen the Lord!"

Women Confused with Mary Magdalene
1. *Luke 7*—the "sinful woman"
   a. Pope Gregory in 591 AD made the connection between the woman of Luke 7 and Mary.
   b. Mary Magdalene has, therefore, been depicted as a prostitute.
2. *Matthew 26* and *John 12*—Mary of Bethany
   a. John 12 identifies the women as Mary.
   b. Jesus was there to see Lazarus and Martha.
   c. Luke 10:30 identifies Mary as the sister of Martha.
   d. There is no reason to connect Mary of Bethany to Mary Magdalene.

Mary's of the New Testament
1. Mary, the mother of Jesus (Luke 1:30–31)
2. Mary, the mother of James (not the Lord's brother) and Joseph (Matthew 27:56)

3. Mary, the sister of Lazarus and Martha (Luke 10:39; John 11:1; John 12:3)
4. Mary, the mother of John Mark (Acts 12:12)
5. Mary, wife of Clopas (or Cleophus) (John 9:25)
6. Unidentified Mary (Romans 16:6)
7. Mary of Magdala, a southwest Galilean city (Luke 8; Matthew 25, 28; and others)

Notes

Chapter 1

1. *Houston Chronicle*, Thursday, December 2, 2004, Section A, 3.
2. *U. S. News and World Report, Collectors Edition*, 2004, 18-19.
3. Ibid.
4. David Klinghoffer, "Religious Fiction," *The National Review*, December 8, 2003.
5. Dan Brown, *The Da Vinci Code (DVC)* (New York: Doubleday, 2003), preface.
6. "Good Morning America," ABC, November 3, 2005.
7. *DVC*, 235.
8. Ibid., 253.
9. Hank Hanegraff and Paul L. Maier, *The Da Vinci Code: Fact or Fiction* (Wheaton, Ill.: Tyndale House, 2004), 8.
10. *DVC*, 234.

11. Ibid., 234.
12. Ibid., 248.
13. John 8:37.
14. *DVC*, 309.
15. Ibid.
16. Carl E. Olson and Sandra Miesel, *The Da Vinci Hoax* (San Francisco: Ignatius Press, 2004), 293.
17. Ibid.
18. Ibid., 294.
19. Ibid.

Chapter 2

1. *DVC*, 232.
2. *DVC*, 253.
3. Michael Baigent, Richard Leigh, and Henry Lincoln, *Holy Blood, Holy Grail* (New York, Random House 2004), 18.
4. Ibid., 19.
5. Ibid., 312.
6. Ibid., 403.
7. Ibid., 363.
8. Margaret Starbird, *The Woman with the Alabaster Jar: Mary Magdalene and the Holy Grail* (Rochester, Vermont: Bear & Company, 1993), xix.
9. Margaret Starbird, *The Goddess in the Gospels: Reclaiming the Sacred Feminine* (Rochester, Vermont: Bear & Company, 1998), 153.
10. Starbird, *The Woman with the Alabaster Jar*, 137.
11. Starbird, *The Goddess of the Gospels*, xi.
12. Ibid., xv.
13. Ibid., 13.
14. Ibid., 12.
15. Ibid., 156.

16. Ibid., 68.
17. Ibid., 77.
18. Ibid., 106.
19. Ibid., 151.
20. Lynn Picknett and Clive Prince, *The Templar Revelation* (New York: Simon & Schuster, 1998), 16.
21. Ibid., 262.
22. Ibid., 237.
23. Ibid., 308.
24. Ibid., 253.
25. Ibid., 63.
26. Ibid., 342.
27. Acts 14:23; Mark 16:16; Luke 16.
28. Picknett and Prince, 287.
29. Ibid., 279, 263.
30. Ibid., 218, 361, 123.
31. Ibid., 261.
32. John 18:36.
33. Matthew 5:44.
34. Dan Burstein, *Secrets of the Code* (New York: CDS Books, 2004), 254.

Chapter 3

1. Burstein, 355.
2. Ibid., 297.
3. Picknett and Prince, 43.
4. Ibid., 44.
5. Baigent, Leigh, and Lincoln, 225.
6. Ibid., 226
7. Darrell L. Brock, *Breaking the Da Vinci Code* (Nashville: Nelson Books, 2004), 85.
8. Ibid., 291.

9. Martin Lunn, *The Da Vinci Code Decoded* (New York: Disinformation, 2004), 47.
10. *National Geographic* television special.
11. *DVC*, 159.
12. Hanegraaff and Maier, 12; Burstein, 163.
13. Simon Cox, *Cracking the Da Vinci Code* (Martinsburg, WV: Barnes and Noble Books, 2004), 119.
14. *DVC*, 138.
15. Olson and Miesel, 261.
16. *DVC*, 244.
17. *Prime Time Monday*, ABC.
18. *DVC*, 248.
19. Burstein, 229.
20. Ibid., 229.

Chapter 4

1. *DVC*, 232, 234.
2. Ephesians 5:23.
3. Matthew 16:18–19.
4. John 18:36.
5. Matthew 3:2.
6. Acts 2.
7. Burstein, 63.
8. Ibid., 65.
9. Ibid., 16.
10. Ibid., 15, 65.
11. Burstein, 18.
12. Bentley Layton, *The Gnostic Scriptures: Ancient Wisdom for the New Age* (New York: Doubleday, 1995), 339.
13. James M. Robinson, ed., *The Nag Hammadi Library* (New York: Harper Collins, 1990), 525.

14. Luke 1:30–31.
15. Matthew 27:56.
16. John 19:25.
17. Luke 10:39; John 11:1; John 12:2.
18. Acts 12:12.
19. Romans 16:6.
20. Matthew 15:39.
21. Burstein, 17.
22. Starbird, *The Woman with the Alabaster Jar*, 51.
23. Albert Barnes, *Notes on the New Testament: Luke and John* (Grand Rapids, Mich.: Baker Book House, 1949), 53; Adam Clarke, *A Commentary and Critical Notes: The New Testament of Our Lord and Saviour Jesus Christ* (New York: Abingdon-Cokesbury Press, 1931), 414–415.
24. Matthew 28:1–8.
25. John 20:13–18.
26. Mathew 28:9–10.
27. Mark 16:9.
28. Matthew 28:9.
29. *DVC*, 248.
30. Ibid., 124.
31. James L. Garlow and Peter Jones, *Cracking Da Vinci's Code* (Colorado Springs: Victor, 2004), 61.
32. Ibid.
33. Plato, Timeas and Critias (London: Penguin Classics, 1965), 58.
34. Genesis 15, 16.
35. Judges 4.
36. Judges 4.
37. Joshua 2.
38. Ruth.
39. Esther.

40. John 4:17–26.
41. Acts 18:26; Romans 16:3.
42. Romans 16:6, 15.
43. Acts 21:9.
44. Galatians 3:28.
45. *DVC*, 125.
46. Garlow and Jones, 66.
47. Kenneth Hanson, *The Dead Sea Scrolls: The Untold Story* (Tulsa, OK: Council Oak Books, 1997), 62.
48. Hebrews 7:14.
49. Hebrews 13:4.
50. Matthew 19:6; Mark 10:9.

Chapter 5

1. *DVC*, 233.
2. Ibid., 231.
3. Ibid., 245.
4. Ibid., 235.
5. Ibid.
6. Norman Davies, *Europe: A History* (New York: Oxford University Press, 1996), 209.
7. *DVC*, 233.
8. Fawn M. Brodie, *No Man Knows My History: The Life of Joseph Smith* (New York: Ventage, 1999), 16–33.
9. Davies, 200.
10. Brock, 118.
11. 1 Corinthians 13:9–10.
12. Colossians 4:16.
13. 2 Peter 3:15–16.
14. 2 Timothy 2:15.
15. Mark 16:20.
16. *DVC*, 232.

17. Josh McDowell, *The New Evidence That Demands a Verdict* (Nashville: Thomas Nelson, 1999), 23.
18. Hanegraaff and Maier, 73.

Chapter 6

1. *DVC*, 234.
2. *DVC*, 245.
3. Bentley Layton, *The Gnostic Scriptures: Ancient Wisdom for the New Age* (New York: Doubleday, 1995), xxvi.
4. Acts, Luke, 1 and 2 Peter.
5. Plato, 121.
6. Ibid., 58.
7. Elaine Pagels, *The Gnostic Gospels* (New York: Ventage Books, 1999), xxi.
8. Layton, 49.
9. 1 John 2.
10. Ibid.
11. 1 John 4:6.
12. 2 John.
13. Robinson, 4; 1 Timothy 2:16–18.
14. Robinson.
15. Layton, xxvi.
16. Ibid., 339.
17. Ibid., 335.
18. Ibid., 338.
19. Ibid., 339.
20. Ibid., 325.
21. Ibid., 345.
22. Ibid., 329.
23. Ibid., 330.
24. Ibid., 331.

25. Ibid., 332.
26. Ibid.
27. Ibid., 342.
28. Ibid., 333.
29. Ibid., 399.
30. Ibid.
31. Ibid., 377.
32. Ibid., 381.
33. Ibid., 383.
34. Ibid., 389.
35. Ibid., 387.
36. Ibid., 392.
37. Ibid., 395.
38. Robinson, 524.
39. Pagels, xxxv.
40. Robinson, 524.
41. Ibid.
42. Ibid., 527.
43. Ibid., 525.
44. Pagels, 35.
45. Ibid., 11.
46. Ibid., 20.
47. Ibid., 11.
48. Ibid., 75.
49. Ibid., 93.
50. Ibid., 98.
51. Ibid., 140–141.
52. Ibid., 142.
53. Ibid., and *DVC*, 233.
54. Picknett and Prince, 134.
55. Layton, 203.
56. Ibid., 207.
57. Ibid., 206.

Chapter 7

1. John Shelby Sponge, *A New Christianity for a New World* (New York: Harper Collins, 2001).
2. Karl Menninger, *Whatever Became of Sin?* (New York: Hawthorne Books, Inc., 1973).
3. Norman Geisler and William E. Nix, *A General Introduction to the Bible* (Chicago: Moody Press, 1986), 28.
4. McDowell, 4–6.
5. www.biblesociety.org.
6. McDowell, 9.
7. Ibid., 13.
8. Ibid.
9. Geisler and Nix, 408.
10. McDowell, 44.
11. Ibid., 55.
12. Seutonious quote from McDowell, 55.
13. 1 Corinthians 15:19.
14. Matthew 26:28.
15. McDowell, 213.
16. Ibid., 218.
17. Matthew 28:11–15.
18. Merrill C. Tenney, *The Reality of the Resurrection* (Chicago: Moody Press, 1963), 119.
19. Paul Little, *Know Why You Believe* (Wheaton, Ill.: Scripture Press, 1987), 173.
20. John R.W. Stott, *Basic Christianity,* 2nd ed. (Downer's Grove, Ill.: Intervarsity Press, 1971), 50.
21. Pagels, 3–27.
22. Smith, Morton396–397.
23. Luke 24:42—43.
24. Matthew 22:66.
25. Mark 15:46.
26. Mark 16:9; John 20:15.

27. John 20:26.
28. John 20:29.
29. Romans 1:4.

<h2>Chapter 8</h2>

1. Pagel, 142.
2. *DVC*, 234.
3. *DVC*, 245.
4. 1 Corinthians 1:10.
5. Jude 4.
6. 2 Peter 2:1.
7. John 17:19–21.
8. Galatians 1:6.
9. Galatians 1:8.
10. Ephesians 5:6.
11. Mark 16:20.
12. 1 Thessalonians 1:3.
13. 1 Corinthians 13:9.
14. Acts 8:18.
15. Acts 9:6.
16. Acts 10.
17. Acts 8:18.
18. Davies, 200.
19. 2 Corinthians 11:15.
20. 2 Corinthians 11:13.
21. 1 Corinthians 15:13–14.
22. 1 Corinthians 15:19.
23. 2 Peter 1:16.
24. Matthew 17:5.
25. 2 Peter 1:18.
26. *DVC*, 231.
27. Ibid.

28. 2 Timothy 3:16.
29. 1 Timothy 1:15.
30. Galatians 2:11.
31. Jude 3.
32. Romans 5:1.
33. Romans 10:17.
34. Hebrews 11:6.
35. 2 Timothy 1:12.
36. 2 Timothy 2:15.
37. Ephesians 4:4.
38. John 8:32.
39. Revelation 22:19.
40. Philippians 2:2.
41. Philippians 2:10.
42. Matthew 18:6.

Appendix I
1. Baigent, Leigh, and Lincoln, 43.
2. Olsen and Miesel, 237.
3. Ibid.

Selected Bibliography

American Broadcasting Company. "Good Morning America." November 3, 2003.

Bahn, Paul G., ed. *The Cambridge Illustrated History of Archaeology*. Cambridge, 1996.

Baigent, Michael; Leigh, Richard; and Lincoln, Henry. *Holy Blood, Holy Grail* (paperback). New York, New York, Random House 2004. (First published 1982.)

Barnes, Albert. *Notes on the New Testament: Luke and John*. Grand Rapids, Mich.: Baker Book House, 1949.

Blomberg, Craig. *The Historical Reliability of the Gospels*. Downers Grove, Ill.: InterVarsity Press, 1987.

Braswell, George W. Jr. *Understanding World Religions*. Nashville: Broadman Press, 1983.

Bock, Darrell L. *Breaking the Da Vinci Code*. Nashville: Nelson Books, 2004.

Brodie, Fawn M. *No Man Knows My History: The Life of Joseph Smith*. New York: Ventage, 1999.

Brown, Dan. *The Da Vinci Code*. New York: Doubleday, 2003.

Bruce. F. F. *The Canon of Scripture*. Downers Grove, Ill: InterVarsity Press, 1988.

Burstein, Dan, ed. *Secrets of the Code*. New York: CDS Books, 2004.

Christian Research Institute. "A Summary Critique—Searching for the Holy Grail—Again, a Book Review of *Holy Blood, Holy Grail*," 2004. (www.equip.org/freeDH228.htm)

Clarke, Adam. *A Commentary and Critical Notes: The New Testament of Our Lord and Saviour Jesus Christ*. New York: Abingdon-Cokesbury Press, 1931.

Cox, Simon. *Cracking the Da Vinci Code*. Martinsburg, WV: Barnes & Noble Books, 2004.

Davies, Norman. *Europe: A History*. New York: Oxford University Press, 1996.

Ehrman, Bart D. *Truth and Fiction in The Da Vinci Code*. New York: Oxford University Press, 2004.

Garlow, James L. and Jones, Peter. *Cracking Da Vinci's Code*. Colorado Springs: Victor, 2004.

Geisler, Norman. *Baker's Encyclopedia of Christian Apologetics*. Grand Rapids, Mich.: Baker Book House, 1998.

Geisler, Norman L. and Nix, William E. *A General Introduction to the Bible*. Chicago: Moody Press, 1986.

Hale, John. *The Civilization of Europe in the Renaissance*. New York: Atheneum, 1993.

Hanegraff, Hank and Maier, Paul L. *The Da Vinci Code: Fact or Fiction*. Wheaton, Ill.: Tyndale House, 2004.

Hanson, Kenneth. The Dead Sea Scrolls: The Untold Story. Tulsa, OK: Council Oak Books, 1997.

Houston Chronicle, Thursday, December 2004.

Jones, A.H.M. *Constantine and the Conversion of Europe*. Toronto: University of Toronto Press, 1978.

King, Karen. *The Gospel of Mary of Magdalene: Jesus and the First Woman Apostle*. 2003.

Klinghoffer, David. "Religious Fiction" *The National Review*. December 8, 2003. New York.

Layton, Bentley. *The Gnostic Scriptures: Ancient Wisdom for the New Age*. New York: Doubleday, 1995 (First Edition 1987).

Little, Paul. *Know Why You Believe*. Wheaton, Ill.: Scripture Press, 1987.

Lunn, Martin. *The Da Vinci Code Decoded*. New York: Disinformation, 2004.

Lutzer, Erwin W. *The Da Vinci Deception*. Wheaton, Ill.: Tyndale House, 2004.

Maguire, Gregory. *Wicked: The Life and Times of the Wicked Witch of the West*. New York: Harper Collins, 1995.

McDowell, Josh. *The New Evidence That Demands a Verdict*. Nashville: Thomas Nelson, 1999.

Menninger, Karl. *Whatever Became of Sin?* New York: Hawthorne Book, Inc., 1973.

Metzger, Bruce. *The Text of the New Testament: Its Trasmission, Corruption and Restoration*. New York: Oxford University Press, 1992.

Miller, David L. *The New Polytheism: Rebirth of God and Goddesses*. New York: Harper and Row, 1974.

National Broadcasting Co., Inc. "Today Show." June 9, 2003.

Newsweek. "How Jesus Became Christ." March 28, 2005.

Olson, Carl E. and Miesel, Sandra. *The Da Vinci Hoax*. San Francisco: Ignatius Press, 2004.

Pagels, Elaine. *The Gnostic Gospels*. New York: Ventage Books, 1999.

Picknett, Lynn and Prince, Clive. *The Templar Revelation*. New York: Simon & Schuster, 1998.

Plato. *Timeas and Critias*. London: Penguin Classics, 1965.

Ramm, Bernard. *Protestant Christian Evidences*. Chicago: Moody Press, 1957.

Read, Paul. *The Templars*. Cambridge: Da Capo Press, 1999.

Robinson, James M., ed. <u>The Nag Hammadi Library</u>. New York: Harper Collins, 1990.

San Antonio Sermons. "The Da Vinci Code: Fact, Fiction and a Few Heresies—An Interview with Dan Brown, 02/08/04." (www.orgsanantonio/sermons/s040208.htm)

Schonfield, Hugh J. *The Passover Plot*. London: Hutchinson, 1965.

Smith, Huston. *The Illustrated World's Religions*. New York: Golden Press, 1994.

Smith, Morton. *Jesus the Magician*. London: Victor Gollanez, 1978.

Smith, Wilbur. *Therefore Stand*. Grand Rapids: Baker Book House, 1945.

Sponge, John Shelby. *A New Christianity for a New World*. New York: Harper Collins, 2001.

Starbird, Margaret. *The Goddess in the Gospels: Reclaiming the Sacred Feminine*. Rochester, Vermont: Bear & Co, 1998.

Starbird, Margaret. *The Woman with the Alabaster Jar: Mary Magdalene and the Holy Grail*. Rochester, Vermont: Bear & Co, 1993.

Stott, John R.W. *Basic Christianity*, 2nd ed. Downers Grove, Ill.: InterVarsity Press, 1971.

Stroble, Lee. *The Case for a Creator*. Grand Rapids, Mich.: Zondervan Publishing, 2004.

Stroble, Lee. *The Case for Christ*. Grand Rapids, Mich.: Zondervan Publishing, 1998.

Tenny, Merrill C. *The Reality of the Resurrection*. Chicago: Moody Press, 1963.

U.S. News & World Report. "Mysteries of the Bible." 2004.

U.S. News & World Report. "Secrets of the Da Vinci Code: The Unauthorized Guide to the Best Selling Novel." 2004.

Vezzosi, Alessandro. *Leonardo DaVinci: The Mind of the Rennaisance*. New York: Harry Abrams, 1997.

Vos, Johannes. *A Christian Introduction to Religions of the World*. Grand Rapids, Mich.: Baker Book House, 1965.

www.biblesociety.org

Whiston, William. *The Complete Works of Josephus. A Translation*. Philadelphia: Kregel Publications, 1981.

Yamauchi, Edwin. *Pre-Christian Gnosticism*. Grand Rapids, Mich.: Wm. B. Eerdmans Publishing Co., 1973.

To order additional copies of
Unveling The Da Vinci Code
have your credit card ready and call
1 800-917-BOOK (2665)

or e-mail
orders@selahbooks.com

or order online at
www.selahbooks.com